DESERT RIVER CROSSING

DESERT RIVER CROSSING

HISTORIC LEE'S FERRY ON THE COLORADO RIVER

W. L. Rusho
C. Gregory Crampton

Peregrine Smith, Inc.

SALT LAKE CITY AND SANTA BARBARA
1975

Library of Congress Cataloging in Publication Data

Rusho, W   L   1928-
    Desert river crossing.

    Bibliography: p.
    Includes index.
    1. Lees Ferry, Ariz.—History. I. Crampton,
Charles Gregory, 1911-   joint author. II. Title.
F819.L44R87   979.1'33   75-22219
ISBN 0-87905-048-9

Manufactured in the United States of America

ACKNOWLEDGMENT

In addition to history gleaned from books, articles, and old records, much information was obtained from still-living participants. Their histories, given through interviews and correspondence, provided much background on Warren M. Johnson, James S. Emett, Charles H. Spencer, and Art Greene. For their generous contributions of knowledge, we wish to thank the following: Frank Johnson, St. George, Utah; Arthur C. Waller, Seattle, Washington; Albert H. Jones, Elizabeth, Colorado; Charles H. Spencer, Riverside, California; Albert Leach, Kanab, Utah; William H. Switzer, Flagstaff, Arizona; Bill Wilson, Clarkdale, Arizona; and Emery Kolb, Grand Canyon, Arizona. Although some of those who contributed information are now deceased, we wish to extend our thanks to their descendants.

Valuable original documents touching on Lee's Ferry history were made available by the Historical Department, Church of Jesus Christ of Latter-day Saints, Salt Lake City; the Utah State Historical Society, Salt Lake City; the Southern California Edison Company, Los Angeles, California; Northern Arizona University, Flagstaff, Arizona; Museum of Northern Arizona, Flagstaff, Arizona; Phoenix Public Library, Phoenix, Arizona; Arizona Department of Archives and Library, Phoenix, Arizona; and Otis "Dock" Marston, San Francisco, California.

Special thanks are due to Dock Marston, noted authority on Colorado River history, for making significant corrections to our manuscript.

In our personal investigations at Lee's Ferry and environs, we were ably assisted by Don Cecala of Salt Lake City, who contributed time, effort, and motorized equipment. Cecala also provided thoughtful suggestions, as well as physical exertions, that helped us to locate historic trails.

CONTENTS

DESERT RIVER CROSSING

FOREWORD

Thirty-five years ago this summer it was my privilege to be accepted as a member of an expedition the late Norman Nevills of Mexican Hat, Utah, led down the Green and Colorado Rivers. Although Nevills' boats were far lighter and more maneuverable than those used by Major John Wesley Powell on his pioneering transit of the river in 1869, and although much had been learned about the river in the intervening years, from the outset of our trip we shared some of the spirit of adventure that had characterized the Powell voyage.

On Thursday, August 1, 1940, we came to Lee's Ferry, our twenty-third camp after I had joined the eight-person party at Green River, Utah. I shall never forget that day. After three weeks in the upper canyons we were back in my native Arizona.

There were many factors to make the day so significant. We were now at Mile Zero on the Colorado, the point from which all distances on the river system are measured, upstream and downstream. For practical purposes this is the division point between the upper and lower basins of the drainage area.

As Will Rusho and Greg Crampton point out admirably in this book, Lee's Ferry was the crossroads and also the center of the riverman's world. It was the gateway into the promised land of refuge for many pioneer Mormons, who found new hope and a brighter future for their families in Arizona Territory. Some of these were "called" to their missions, while others sought to increase the distance from increasing pressure of prosecution faced by the Latter-day Saints in Utah for their plural marriage practices.

For some who found the arid lands of northern Arizona too difficult for colonization, Lee's Ferry was a memorable place on the return to home and family in Utah. Here the settled Arizona colonists crossed the river on the Honeymoon Trail leading to St. George, Utah, for ordinations and marriage in the L.D.S. Temple there. For Navajos and Utes, as well as for all manner of white travelers, Lee's Ferry was the only acceptable crossing point along hundreds of miles of the turbulent Colorado.

In modern times, it has marked the start for river journeys through the lower forges of the Colorado, one of the last memorable adventures still available in a shrinking world.

This book occupies a unique place in the annals of the Colorado River; none other has dealt directly with the long series of fascinating historical events that occurred at Lee's Ferry.

Beautiful, historic, restful—Lee's Ferry always has been one of my favorite spots in my native, my favorite state.

Senator Barry M. Goldwater

3

1 A POINT OF VIEW

In its long plunge to the sea, the Colorado River has cut its canyons through one upraised plateau after another, almost like deep grooves down through a giant staircase. In some places, where the river exits one canyon and before it enters another, a relatively short open area appears. Such a place is Lee's Ferry,[1] located between Glen Canyon upstream and Marble Canyon downstream. For a stretch of about two miles at Lee's Ferry one can reach the river's edge from either bank.

In spite of this available access to the river, Lee's Ferry is far from being a level place. Visitors are confronted with a magnificent but bewildering array of cliffs, rocky pinnacles, rough mesas and gulches that seem to defy understanding.

All of the massive exposures of rock strata are sedimentary in origin, having been laid down as water deposits, or solidified from arid sand dunes. Geologists say that the rocks visible about Lee's Ferry were formed during the Paleozoic and Mesozoic eras about 250 to 150 million years ago. For example, the highway into Lee's Ferry runs across the Kaibab limestone formation that is 225 million years old—a period of time that is almost beyond human comprehension.[2]

If the age of the rocks is mind-boggling, it may be a little easier to understand that it has taken the Colorado River, its antecedent streams, and its tributaries only about 20 million years to cut through the sedimentary strata to form the present landscape.

And what a landscape! Nearly every first-time visitor to Lee's Ferry is left breathless by the engulfing grandeur of the scenery. Steep, rough, and broken cliffs soar to heights of two to three thousand feet above the river. Between them the desert river, the Colorado, dramatically breaks through the long wall of the Echo Cliffs, tumbles over the broad boulder delta at the mouth of the Paria River, then plunges into the jagged gorge of Marble Canyon. Indeed, Lee's Ferry is one of the most starkly beautiful places in the entire canyon country of the Colorado River.

None has appreciated it more than Theodore Roosevelt, who rode through on a pack trip in 1912. He wrote:

> The landscape had become of incredible wildness, of tremendous and desolate majesty. No one could paint or describe it save one of the great masters of imaginative art or literature—a Turner or

Browning or Poe. The sullen rock walls towered hundreds of feet aloft, with something about their grim savagery that suggested both the terrible and the grotesque. The cliffs were channeled into myriad forms—battlements, spires, pillars, buttressed towers, flying arches; they looked like the ruined castles and temples of the monstrous devil—deities of some vanished race. All were ruins—ruins vaster than those of any structures ever neared by the hands of men—as if some magic city, built by warlocks and sorcerers, had been wrecked by the wrath of the elder gods....At Lee's Ferry, once the home of the dark leader of the Danites, the cliffs, a medley of bold colors and striking forms, come close to the river's brink on either side; but at this one point there is a break in the canyon walls and a ferry can be run.[3]

Men react differently to the almost overpowering cliffs, crags, peaks, and mesas, and to the desert and the desert river. Some see the terrain as bleak and hostile, but most, like Theodore Roosevelt, see a landscape of radiant beauty, capable of lifting the thoughts and deeds of men.

From the pages of history, this diversity of reactions is expressed:

It has an agreeably confused appearance.

Fray Vélez de Escalante, 1776

[Lee's Ferry] is desolate enough to suit a lovesick poet.

Jack Sumner of Powell's 1869 Expedition

Oh, what a lonely dell!

Emma Lee, 1871

I saw the constricted rapids, where the Colorado took its plunge into the box-like head of the Grand Cañon of Arizona; and the deep, reverberating boom of the river, at flood height, was a fearful thing to hear. I could not repress a shudder at the thought of crossing above that rapid.

Zane Grey, in THE LAST OF THE PLAINSMEN, *1908*

We dropped down over a lot of hills that seemed made out of all the scrapings of the Painted Desert and saw a big copper line like a badly twisted snake crawling along below with the greenest fields I ever saw beyond it and the reddest cliffs behind them.... It was as beautiful as it was wild and strange and I doubt if there is a wilder, stranger spot in the Southwest.

Sharlot Hall, Arizona State Historian, 1911

Geographically our 42nd and Broadway lies exactly in the center of [the Colorado River Basin]. Like Times Square, it has its popular name—Lee's Ferry. For nearly four centuries everybody has eventually showed up here at the confluence of the Colorado and the Paria.

Frank Waters in THE COLORADO, *1946*

The Colorado River, flowing left to right, breaks through the Echo Cliffs at Lee's Ferry. The Paria River flows from lower right past Lee's Ferry Ranch. The sharp river bend at left was the main ferry site, used from 1873 to 1928. *Courtesy Bureau of Reclamation*

2 THE FIRST MEN

Thousands of years ago the first men reached the banks of the Colorado River, but no one can say exactly where, or when, this occurred. Evidence of an early human inhabitant—perhaps the first in the area—has been found in the canyon country not far from Lee's Ferry.

About thirty miles downstream, in Marble Canyon, river runners and archaeologists have found a number of small animal figurines made of split willow twigs. When radiocarbon dated, these figurines were discovered to be an astonishing four thousand years old. Lack of any associated material, however, has left many questions about their makers.[1]

Artifacts from a still older Indian culture have been dug up near Navajo Mountain, about forty miles to the northeast. During the early 1960s, archaeologists from the Museum of Northern Arizona sifted through shallow caves and unearthed woven sandals made from yucca leaves that registered an age of between seven and eight thousand years. These early dates surprised even the scientists. Situated with the sandals were projectile points, knives, grinding slabs, and other artifacts. These items, together with an associated large number of small mammal bones, have led archaeologists to conclude that this group of Indians subsisted on wild plant foods and small game, with large game serving as a rare treat. To these ancient inhabitants of Navajo Mountain, and to their artifacts, scientists have bestowed the name Desha Complex.[2]

It is quite probable that the men of the Desha Complex and those who made the split twig figurines both belonged to what is known as the Desert Culture. More abundant evidence of Desert Man has been found in the Great Basin portions of Utah and Nevada. Desert Man seems to have disappeared from the canyon country. Either his descendants evolved into later Indian cultures in the same area or he migrated to other regions.

By the dawn of the Christian Era, a new group of Indians was living on the mesas near Lee's Ferry. These were the Basketmakers, who eventually learned to make pottery and were known thereafter as the Pueblos. Their culture is known generally as Anasazi, from the Navajo word for "ancient ones." They did not depend exclusively on hunting and wild food gathering but obtained much of their subsistence from cultivated crops, such as corn or squash.

From physical evidence, it would appear that the Anasazi population was light at first; then it increased dramatically beginning about 1000 A.D. For the next one hundred fifty years this group built many stone and adobe structures to serve as dwellings, storage bins, and ceremonial rooms. Some of these structures were built as cliff dwellings within the canyons, but the greater number were constructed on the high rimlands.

To judge from evidence so far uncovered, Anasazi occupation of the immediate Lee's Ferry area, despite the easy availability of water and farm land, was light. A few years ago, archaeologists from the Museum of Northern Arizona located two small ruins near the mouth of the Paria River. These were dated about 1100 to 1150 A.D.[3] On top of a hill near the Paria, known locally as Lee's Lookout, a circle of rocks appears to be of prehistoric origin. Petroglyphs, symbols incised on rock surfaces, have been found in some number along the Paria River within three miles of its mouth. Perhaps additional evidence of Anasazi occupation of the Lee's Ferry area will be found, but no competent, systematic investigation has ever been made.

Even if prehistoric ruins are scarce at Lee's Ferry, many Anasazi ruins

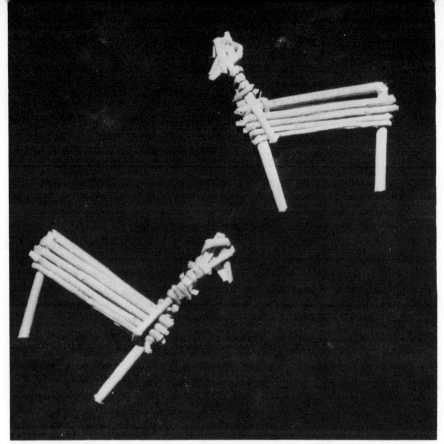

Split twig figurines, made by prehistoric Indians 4,000 years ago, were found in Marble Canyon caves.

can be found on the high Paria Plateau, outlined by the spectacular Vermilion Cliffs immediately to the west. The population density of the Anasazi on the Paria Plateau may have been fairly high, for on the Kaiparowits Plateau, a similar highland to the northeast, archaeologists have found ten Anasazi dwelling sites per square mile.

Near the turn of the thirteenth century the Anasazi abandoned the canyon country. Either suddenly or over a number of years a mass exodus took place. For what reason no one can say with certainty, but geologists have pointed to an intensive soil erosion cycle that began about the year 1250. A long drouth, which has been verified from tree ring data, probably dried the streams and fields. Natural cover vegetation withered and died, leaving the land open to the devastating force of brief but torrential cloudbursts. Cornfields were slashed by deep gullies as the topsoil was washed into the Colorado River.

Other factors, such as pressure from encroaching Indian tribes moving in from the north, may have given additional reason for vacating the region. Most authorities believe that the Anasazi bands then in northern

Arizona and southern Utah moved south, where their descendants are now known as Hopis.

Not long—possibly a hundred years—after the departure of the "ancient ones" from the canyon country, the ancestors of modern Indians moved in. These were the Southern Paiutes, close relatives of the Utes. It is even possible that the Southern Paiutes may have helped force the Anasazi into exodus. Fragmentary evidence indicates that by the fourteenth century Paiutes were in the vicinity of Lee's Ferry, although their numbers were few.

Primitive in the extreme, the Paiutes did little else than spend their entire waking hours searching for food: seeds, rabbits, mice, or birds. Even insects were part of their diet. Deer were occasionally hunted on the plateaus.

Only on rare occasions would the Paiutes' hunting forays have taken them to the mouth of the Paria. If they desired to cross the Colorado River, which was probably seldom, they would have chosen a place where swimming or wading was a little safer. Such places were to be found farther upstream.

Although Lee's Ferry today borders on the Navajo Reservation, no evidence indicates that the Navajos lived along the Colorado River prior to about 1850. Sometime before 1500 A.D. they migrated from the north, settling in the Chuska Mountains near the present Arizona-New Mexico border. From this base they gradually extended their domain westward to the Colorado River. In the 1860s they ran headlong into the eastward and southward-moving frontier of the Mormons.[4]

3 THROUGH AN UNKNOWN LAND

Because they had found a spring of cool water at the base of a desert cliffside, they had named their last camp San Fructo. Now they were on their way again, urging their horses through the rolling sands and gravels at the base of the same long cliff, heading northeast toward what they thought would be an exit from the valley. Only when they neared the supposed exit did they realize that the valley was virtually surrounded by steep, arid cliffs of broken red rock. Thus did the first white men of European ancestry see what would later be called Lee's Ferry. The date was October 26, 1776.[1]

Leading the group of horsemen were two Spanish priests—Fray Francisco Atanasio Domínguez and Fray Silvestre Vélez de Escalante.

Domínguez was nominally in charge, but Escalante kept the written journal, and it is from his book that the expedition is generally known—the Escalante Expedition.

Late in July of 1776 the explorers had left Santa Fe hoping to find a northern trail through to Monterey in California. If their late departure did not allow them time enough to reach their objective, they would at least learn more about the northern tribes. They could also study the geography of the land.

Traveling northwest into present-day Colorado they left previously explored routes to venture forth into *tierra incognita,* heading generally north, then west into what is now Utah. At Utah Lake they turned south to reach the latitude of Monterey before continuing on a westward course.

As they plodded through the rough dry land near present-day Cedar City, they were struck by an early winter storm. Hundreds of miles still lay between them and the Pacific coast, yet already snow was in the air. A dramatic "casting of lots" decided that they should return to Santa Fe. Since they had reached their location by a circuitous route, they chose to return by a more direct—but unexplored—route.

Traveling south beyond the Virgin River, the Spaniards then turned east across the present Arizona Strip, hoping to find a ford across the Colorado River. With no one to guide them they had to rely on vague information supplied by itinerant Indians. About all they could learn was that somewhere to the northeast a ford did exist.

When they reached the Lee's Ferry area they quickly realized that it was not the ford. Even worse, perhaps they had ridden into a giant cul-de-sac with no easy escape. They named their camp San Benito, then added "Salisipuedes," which means "get out if you can!" Located beside the Colorado at the base of a high rock, their campsite is easily identifiable today (see Tour Section, Site No. 7). The nearby Paria River was given the name Rio Santa Teresa.

Even if this was not the ford the Spaniards were looking for, they felt that perhaps a crossing could be made. Two of the men, naked, carrying their clothes on their heads, swam across, but the river was so swift and wide that they lost their clothes and were too weak to explore the opposite bank. Although the men managed to recross, Domínguez and Escalante gave up all thought of swimming.

Several days later Escalante built a crude raft and set out to pole his way across the river. But he could not touch bottom with the pole, and contrary winds kept blowing him back to shore. With this failure the padres at last realized that they lacked both the knowledge and the equipment needed to cross their men at Lee's Ferry. Somehow, they must find a way out of this cliff-bound river bottom.

About three miles up the Paria one of the expedition members had

11

discovered a place where the rugged cliffs to the east might be climbed. Although Escalante and Domínguez were at first hesitant to try this climb, they finally agreed that it was their only choice. On November 2, up they went, over the steep, rocky, sometimes sandy, two thousand-foot high slope. In his journal, Escalante described the climb: "We spent more than three hours in climbing it because at the beginning it is very rugged and sandy and afterward has very difficult stretches and extremely perilous ledges of rock, and finally it becomes almost impassable" (see Tour Site No. 10).[2]

Since this pass over the cliffs has no official name, we will refer to it as Domínguez Pass, in honor of the leader of the expedition. Domínguez Pass was used in later years and will be mentioned again in this account.

When the expedition members finally crested the cliffs, they proceeded through rough gulches then turned northeast across more open, sandy country. That night they camped beside a small stream that was saline but fit to drink. Across from their camp Escalante noted "little mesas and peaks of red earth which at first sight look like the ruins of a fortress." The expedition was, in fact, on the banks of Wahweap Creek, near the place where Wahweap Lodge and Marina stand today. Across the bay are the rocky "ruins."

In desperation they spent two days trying to cross the Colorado at the mouth of Navajo Creek, only to fail and push on. Finally, on November 6, the long-sought ford was sighted, and on November 7, the expedition made its way down Padre Creek Canyon to the Colorado River, which was crossed diagonally without having to swim. In high spirits, Escalante wrote, "We praised God our Lord and fired off a few muskets as a sign of the great joy which we all felt at having overcome so great a difficulty which had cost us so much labor and delay."

With some further effort they traversed the intricate canyon country east of the river, but once past White Mesa they traveled through more open terrain by way of the Hopi villages and Zuni Pueblo. They arrived back in Santa Fe on January 2, 1777.

The ford that Escalante and Domínguez found had been used by Indians, perhaps for centuries. After 1776 it was used for about another 100 years, or until the ferry at Lee's Ferry became a reliable operation. The historic ford was eventually abandoned but not forgotten. It went on the maps, appropriately enough, with two names: Ute Ford commemorates the Indian usage, and Crossing of the Fathers (as it is usually called) commemorates Domínguez and Escalante. Crossing of the Fathers lies about forty river miles above Lee's Ferry and twenty-five miles above Glen Canyon Dam. It is now covered to a great depth by the waters of Lake Powell.

Wilderness closed swiftly upon the wake of the Escalante expedition. After 1776 the Spanish crown practically ignored the region north and

Crossing of the Fathers as seen from the air, before inundation by Lake Powell. On November 7, 1776, Domínguez and Escalante led their party, on horseback, into Padre Creek (lower right), then to the Colorado River. They crossed diagonally near the wide bend at right center. *Courtesy Bureau of Reclamation*

west of New Mexico. Although one Mexican trading caravan on the way to California forded at Crossing of the Fathers in 1829, most travelers preferred less arduous routes.[3] After 1831 the Old Spanish Trail, which headed the canyons through more open lands in central Utah, carried virtually all the traffic.

In the early 1800s the United States, having declared its independence in the same year that Domínguez and Escalante were in the field, was spreading its influence to the west. Among the first Americans to reach the Rocky Mountains were the beaver trappers or mountain men, who worked mainly near the headwaters. But beaver were found—and probably trapped—along the Colorado clear to its mouth. It can be assumed that wherever there were beaver there were at least occasional visits by mountain men, even though few records indicate trapping along the Colorado.

One recorded journey into the canyon country was made by James Ohio Pattie, who in 1826 traveled the rimlands of the Colorado from the Gila River north and east to the present state of Colorado.[4] Pattie's descriptions, however, are so imprecise that reconstructing his route is mostly guesswork; he may or may not have seen the site of Lee's Ferry.

Denis Julien, another enigmatic mountain man, "recorded" his presence in canyons of the Green and Colorado Rivers by cutting his name on the rock walls. His last inscription was placed in Cataract Canyon, 180 miles above Lee's Ferry. If Julien was boating, which is probable, and if he didn't drown in a rapid, he may have trapped beaver all the way through Glen Canyon.[5]

If for seventy years after Domínguez and Escalante Lee's Ferry was seen by few, if any, non-Indians, by the 1850s new forces were shaping that would bring the lonely spot into historical prominence.

4 MORMON CROSSING

Expansion of the Mormon frontier outward from Salt Lake City after 1847 was the result of a determination by leaders of the Church of Jesus Christ of Latter-day Saints to extend the Mormon spiritual and temporal realm through all valleys and mountains still unoccupied by white men. Under the vigorous direction of Brigham Young, president of the Church, members participated in a cooperative planned colonization. They were remarkably successful in extending their frontiers, even into the desert country of the Colorado Plateau.

Mormon colonization early developed a strong southward bent, a trend that continued for many years. Mindful of the importance of an ice-free river route to the Pacific, as well as of the desirability of colonization in warm climes, the Latter-day Saints founded the first permanent settlements in southern Utah, southern Nevada, and northern Arizona. A cluster of settlements on the rim of the Great Basin and along the middle reaches of the Virgin River in southwestern Utah—Parowan, Cedar City, Santa Clara, St. George, and others, all settled in the years between 1850 and 1861—became the nucleus for further expansion southward into Nevada and California as well as eastward toward the Colorado River and central Arizona.

In the Book of Mormon, Indians were called "Lamanites," an errant people who had fallen from the faith in the ancient past. One of the first efforts in any new area was therefore missionary activity to bring the Indian inhabitants back into the fold. Successful missionary work would not only save souls; it would lessen resistance to incoming settlers. In the Mormon view, peaceful conversion was far better than violent confrontation.

In addition to propagating the faith among Utah's Utes and Paiutes, Latter-day Saints took an early interest in the Hopi Indians living south-

14

east across the Colorado River. It had been reported to them that Hopis lived in towns, supported themselves by farming, and were peaceful.

In 1858 Jacob Hamblin, already known locally as an Indian missionary, was sent by the Church to find out. With a party of twelve men, Hamblin headed east for the Hopi villages, guided by a Paiute, Naraguts, who claimed he knew how to reach the old Ute Ford across the Colorado.[1]

As they neared the river, Hamblin and his men unknowingly retraced Escalante's footsteps. They too rode through House Rock Valley, looked up at the towering Vermilion Cliffs, and arrived at the mouth of the Paria River. Naraguts at length recognized his error; this was not the ford. The confused guide then led the party up the Paria to the only point where the cliffs to the east could be climbed—undoubtedly the same point reached in 1776 by the Spanish padres—Domínguez Pass (see Tour Site No. 10). When they finally located the Crossing of the Fathers the Mormon missionaries forded the river and rode south to the Hopi villages without further trouble.

As it turned out, about the last thing the Hopis wanted was proselyting missionaries. Preferring their own religion, the Hopis had turned deaf ears to preachments of Catholic fathers based in New Mexico (including Escalante) and had even excluded them from their mesa-top villages. Jacob Hamblin and his men were politely received by the Hopis, but these Indians gave no indication that they were ready to embrace a new faith. After a visit of a few days the discouraged Mormons returned home.

A year later, in 1859, Brigham Young ordered another missionary attempt, again sending Jacob Hamblin and six others to the Hopis. Following the same route as the previous year, the party reached the mouth of the Paria where one of the members, Thales Haskell, took note of apparent natural resources. The Paria, he wrote in his diary, was a good-sized stream that might be used to irrigate crops planted along its banks. Camped that evening at the base of the cliffs, Haskell wrote, "We spread out our meat—ate a hearty supper—sang songs—hobbled the animals and went to bed. Plenty of water, grass, and cottonwood at this place."[2]

On this second mission the Hopis were noticeably less friendly and the Mormons accomplished little. Two men stayed through the winter, but the Hopis would not listen to their preachings. The undaunted Hamblin, however, made plans for yet a third trip to Hopiland in 1860. Because the Hopis had refused to supply even minimal sustenance to the uninvited Mormons, he carried along enough food and other essentials on the trip to last the missionaries a full year.

Hamblin realized that if the men and their baggage could be ferried across the Colorado at the mouth of the Paria, they would eliminate much rough travel and would save considerable time. Accordingly, the expedition started out with a sixteen-foot boat loaded on a wagon. Both boat and wagon, however, were left behind when the trail became too rough. Upon reaching the mouth of the Paria they constructed a crude raft, hoping to use it to ferry the Colorado. A few men barely made it across, a horse was drowned, and they concluded that it was too dangerous an undertaking. They mounted their horses and proceeded over Domínguez Pass toward the Crossing of the Fathers.

On this 1860 trip the Mormons had their first encounter with Navajo Indians—and it was a violent one. On November 1, 1860, near the present trading post at Tonalea, Hamblin's party was accosted by a group of defiant Navajos who finally agreed to leave the Mormons in peace if they would give up some of the trade goods originally intended for the Hopis. This done, the Mormons went on their way, all except George A. Smith, Jr., who went back to retrieve a horse and became separated from his party. Two Navajos rode up to Smith and asked to see his revolver. Smith complied, only to be shot three times with his own gun.

Hamblin and the others returned and rescued Smith, who was in great pain and asked only that he be allowed to die in peace. Meanwhile the Indians gathered about in a threatening mood. Discarding all thought of going on to the Hopis, the Mormons turned back to Utah.

Smith managed to ride until sundown, when he asked Hamblin to stop. A few minutes later he died beside the trail. His body was wrapped in a blanket and hidden under a rock ledge, after which the surviving Mormons made haste for Utah, riding far into the night. A few months later, in mid-winter, Hamblin and a small group returned to the spot and recovered Smith's remains. George A. Smith, Jr. was the first casualty in a conflict of two expanding frontiers as Mormons moving south and east ran into Navajos moving northwest toward the Colorado River.

As a result of repeated raids on New Mexico settlements, Navajos in 1860 found themselves practically at war with the United States Army. To escape military expeditions sent against them, the more recalcitrant tribesmen began moving into the canyon country of the Colorado. Warfare with the Navajos finally culminated in an intensive army campaign in 1863 and 1864 that concluded with a Navajo surrender. All Navajos that could be found were then marched to Bosque Redondo in central New Mexico—the so-called "Long Walk." Many of the more belligerent Navajos, however, escaped the round-up by fleeing to the remote canyons of the north, joining those that had gone there earlier.

For Utah's Mormon settlements, a growing population of Navajos just across the Colorado only spelled trouble. As had been feared, the Indians soon began making raids into Utah, driving off hundreds of cattle, horses, and mules. During this period, whenever southern Utah settlers had trouble with Indians, they called on Jacob Hamblin. On this occasion Hamblin was asked to warn the Navajos to stop making raids into Utah. Hamblin and his party of fourteen men reached the mouth of the Paria River on March 22, 1864. As in 1860, they built a raft, but this time they made it across the Colorado with all the men and baggage. They swam the horses behind the raft. Thus they made the first successful river crossing at the point later to become Lee's Ferry.[3]

As it turned out this spring trip of 1864 was unfruitful, since no Navajos could be found. In the fall of the same year Hamblin tried again, once more rafting the river at Lee's Ferry, but this effort also failed to uncover Navajos.

Although Jacob Hamblin couldn't find them, the Navajos were close enough to continue raiding into Utah. Aware of their exposed southeastern frontier, the Mormons in 1865 put up a fort at Kanab. For isolated settlers the situation became highly critical when nearby Paiute Indians also started making raids. In 1866 widespread Indian raids and killings so alarmed Mormon authorities that they ordered the abandonment of remote outposts, including the new fort at Kanab. Travel between villages was cut to a minimum, while areas near the Indians were avoided altogether. Scattered fights occurred through the 1860s, but there were no major encounters.

One effect of the "war" was that Mormon militiamen, while on patrol, looked over much of the land to the east of their settlements, and, on occasion, found small areas suitable for farming. On one such military foray in March 1869, a force of thirty-six militiamen crested the Echo Cliffs near Domínguez Pass, affording them a magnificent view of cliffs, canyons, and river bottoms around the present Lee's Ferry. The campaigners reported favorably on the area, stating that it might be a good place to cross the Colorado and that successful farming might be conducted beside the Paria.[4]

Although the Navajo Treaty of 1868 permitted all tribesmen to return to their homelands, scattered raids into Utah continued, but with less frequency.

In October 1869, Jacob Hamblin, with a well-armed force of fifty-nine men, made another fruitless attempt to locate Navajos and give them a warning. More explicit this time, he states in his autobiography, "we crossed the Colorado where Lee's Ferry now is. Our luggage went over on rafts made of floatwood fastened together with withes." When he could find no Navajos he and his men went on to visit the comparatively friendly Hopis.

Later that same October, Hamblin posted Mormon guards at the Crossing of the Fathers and at the "Pahreah Crossing," as Lee's Ferry was then called, to watch for marauding Navajos. Throughout the winter of 1869-1870, Hamblin supervised the activities of sentries at both points.

Guards at the Pahreah Crossing built a small stone building and a corral and named it "Fort Meeks," in honor of the elected leader of the camp, William Meeks. Situated against a high rock wall, Fort Meeks was probably quite close to the Escalante campsite of 1776 (see Tour Site No. 7).

In February, 1870, Jacob Hamblin roughed out a farm along the Paria. With the help of nine Paiutes, he cleared some land, dug an irrigation ditch a mile and a half from an upstream bend of the river, and sowed wheat seed. Much of the work was done, Jacob wrote, "with a gun strapped on my back in case of a sudden attack by Navajos."[5]

Apparently the venture did not succeed, for the farm was not mentioned in any other diary or journal for that period. Jacob Hamblin's account is all that is known about the farm on the Paria. By 1869, however, Mormons had begun to realize the importance of Lee's Ferry, particularly in regard to their dealings with Navajos. But that same spot had seen other, quite dissimilar, activity that same year, for it was in the year 1869 that a group of men first boated through these canyons. Their leader's name was Major John Wesley Powell.

5 MAJOR POWELL DISCOVERS LEE'S FERRY

Thunderstorms played across the canyons around Lee's Ferry during the late afternoon of August 4, 1869, hurling wind, lightning bolts, and rain from a dark gray sky. But as evening came on, the clouds scattered and the wind stilled.

On an upstream bend of the river three dark shapes appeared. An observer might have made out three boats carrying nine strange-looking men. All were thin and haggard, their clothes merely a collection of torn and dirty rags. Near the mouth of the Paria, they pulled into shore on the right bank. A bearded, one-armed man stepped from his boat and stated that camp for the night would be made at that point.

Leading the expedition was John Wesley Powell, then a professor of geology at Illinois Wesleyan University. As a Union officer in the Civil War he had lost his right forearm at the Battle of Shiloh. (Although he was discharged with the rank of Brevet Lieutenant Colonel, he used the

Major John Wesley Powell, government scientist, who explored the Colorado River in 1869 and 1871-72.

title of "Major" the rest of his life). In 1869 he was little known, but his curiosity, solid competence, and driving ambition were soon to make his name known throughout the United States. One might say that his road to fame was the Colorado River.[1]

Powell had made summer expeditions to the Colorado Rockies in 1867 and 1868, and had, while there, conceived a basic plan to study canyon geology by boating down the Green and Colorado Rivers. The purpose of the 1869 trip was only superficially scientific. Powell's real intent was to learn whether men in boats could actually navigate the river. Rather than scientists, Powell chose for his crew bullwhackers, hunters, an army sergeant, and frontier newspapermen. These were men who were accustomed to outdoor hardships and who apparently knew how to survive in the wilderness. Science could wait. Notably lacking among the crew were experienced boatmen.

On May 24, 1869, the party left Green River, Wyoming, in heavy, cumbersome boats that Powell imagined would be ideal. In the six hundred-mile long chain of river canyons above Lee's Ferry, they survived a two-month series of major and minor accidents.

On the morning of August 4, while in the lower part of Glen Canyon, the voyagers passed the Crossing of the Fathers, which Powell recognized as the "Ute Trail." It was late afternoon of the same day when they reached the mouth of the Paria. One of the men, Jack Sumner, climbed the hill known today as Lee's Lookout, on top of which he noted the remains of an "old Indian Fort" (see Tour Site No. 6). Of the entire area, Sumner wrote in his diary that it was "desolate enough to suit a lovesick poet."[2] Crewmember George Y. Bradley noted in his diary that at the "Pah Rhear River, [there is] a small trail where the Mormons have a ferry."[3]

Departing early the next morning, the voyagers began the long run through Grand Canyon. Narrow escapes, continual hardships, and shortage of food culminated in the departure of three men who chose to climb out, hoping to reach the Mormon settlements rather than face what appeared to be certain death in the canyon. They gambled and lost. Brothers Oramel and Seneca Howland and William Dunn were killed, reportedly by Indians, on the high Shivwits Plateau not far from the rim of Grand Canyon. Meanwhile, reduced to six men, the boating party finished the trip through the canyon.

A year later Major Powell was back, not to boat the river but to plan a more extensive second voyage. He particularly wanted to find points along the river where supplies for the boaters could be brought in by pack train.

In Salt Lake City Powell met with Brigham Young, who not only pledged his cooperation but offered to explore part of the country with Powell. The agreed-upon expedition got underway in early September,

A woodcut from Powell's report depicts an 1872 lunch stop in Marble Canyon, a few miles below Lee's Ferry.

1870, when Powell and Young, joined by about forty other Mormons, rode east across southern Utah high plateaus into the upper reaches of the Paria River. Jacob Hamblin was the guide.[4]

One of the important Mormons traveling with Young, Hamblin, and Powell was John D. Lee. During the week-long trip Lee had many conversations with Young about Lee's future in the southern settlements. Lee also talked frequently with Major Powell. A favorite topic of their discussions was the strange rocky land through which they were passing. Brigham Young was disgusted at the general barrenness of the Paria Valley, declaring, "There is nothing here desirable for us." Apparently he did not notice the scenery.

From the Paria, Young's party went to Kanab Fort, where the future town was laid out, then on to Pipe Springs, where Brigham and others made plans to construct a fort. The fort at Pipe Springs, today a national monument, served both as a defensive post on the frontier and as headquarters for the operation of a Mormon livestock cooperative.

Leaving Pipe Springs with Jacob Hamblin, Major Powell headed southwest to learn the fate of the three men who had climbed out of Grand Canyon the year before. At a later campfire conference with the Shivwits Indians, Powell's inquiry was pressed by Hamblin, who acted as interpreter. As later reported by Powell, the tribesmen admitted killing the three men but claimed it was a case of mistaken identity.[5]

Meanwhile, two of Powell's men loaded lumber onto a mule train and headed for the mouth of the Paria. Their orders were to build a

Major Powell and Jacob Hamblin (right side of campfire) confer with Shivwits Indians on the Arizona Strip, north of the Grand Canyon. *Courtesy National Archives*

flatboat that could be used to cross the river. Christened the *Cañon Maid,* this scow was the first real boat used at Lee's Ferry as a ferryboat.[6]

Powell probably first realized how important Lee's Ferry was as an access point when he and Hamblin arrived September 30, 1870. On October 2, Powell and Hamblin, together with eight Mormon men, boated across the river and headed south. Within the next month they visited the Hopi villages and went on to Fort Defiance, where Jacob Hamblin concluded a peace treaty with the Navajos. From Fort Defiance Major Powell boarded a stagecoach and headed east to make final arrangements for his next river trip.

Powell embarked in May 1871 from Green River, Wyoming, to float through the canyons again. For the 1871 crew, instead of hunters and frontiersmen, Powell assembled a group of reasonably competent topographers, geologists, an artist, and a photographer, as well as a cook and general helpers. The only outstanding member, however, was Powell's own brother-in-law, Almon Harris Thompson, the chief topographer. Aside from Powell and Thompson, most of the men were green and inexperienced, but their skills later developed sharply under heavy demands of field work. As in 1869, none in the crew could claim any substantial experience as a boatman.[7]

Since Powell could count on bringing horses and supplies to the mouth of the Paria, he planned to terminate the 1871 leg of the trip at that point. His men would spend the winter in southern Utah. Following this plan, the expedition moved slowly down the Green and Colorado, not arriving in lower Glen Canyon until October. Powell, impatient as usual, skipped part of the run on the Green River, rejoined his men, then left the trip at the Crossing of the Fathers while his men boated on down to the Paria.

On October 21, within sight of their goal, Thompson, Frederick Dellenbaugh, and Francis M. Bishop climbed the cluster of rugged peaks southwest of their camp. On top, Dellenbaugh tried to hit the distant river with a shot from his Remington 44 revolver. The deafening roar was followed by a silence of twenty-four seconds. Then, Dellenbaugh reported, the sound echoed back with a "rattle like that of musketry." Their perch was named on the spot—the Echo Peaks. From these high points a long line of cliffs runs from the lower valley of the Paria, is bisected by the Colorado, then extends southward about sixty miles to the Indian village of Moenave. Taking the name from the peaks, the line of cliffs became known as the Echo Cliffs (see Tour Site No. 17).[8]

From their vantage point 2400 feet above the river, the explorers enjoyed magnificent vistas of the canyon country all about them: to the south the Painted Desert bordered by the Echo Cliffs and the jagged gash of Marble Canyon, and in the distance, the San Francisco peaks; to the northeast Glen Canyon, in the distance separating the Kaiparowits

Plateau and Navajo Mountain; to the southwest the forest-capped Kaibab Plateau; and to the northwest, directly in front of them, the spectacular Vermilion Cliffs bordering the Paria Plateau.

When Powell's men made camp in the tall willows at the mouth of the Paria on October 23, the 1871 leg of the second river trip came to an end. Five days later they used their boats to ferry Jacob Hamblin and his men, who were returning from another trip to the Navajo country. With Hamblin were nine visiting Navajos who entertained the whites all that evening with songs and dances.

Powell's men remained at the Paria, waiting for a pack train with supplies, which finally arrived several days late. Apparently the two men with the pack train knew of Domínguez Pass but couldn't recognize it. They had wandered along the rim of the cliff overlooking the Paria for days before they finally found the trail. By then the animals were practically dead of thirst.

The supplies not needed until the next summer were cached, while the boats were taken above high water marks and concealed. On November 6, 1871, Powell's men left the mouth of the Paria and traveled to Kanab, where they set up a base camp that was used as headquarters for a winter survey of parts of southern Utah and the Arizona Strip.

In June 1872, Thompson and some of the men made a difficult traverse across canyon tributaries of Glen Canyon from the upper Paria to the Dirty Devil River. A central objective was to obtain geographical information about the intricately eroded canyon country, but they also sought to recover one of their boats that had been left at the mouth of nearby North Wash in 1871. After reaching their objective, four men were detailed to take the boat down to the mouth of the Paria and to take photographs on the way. The others made their way overland.

From the point of view of the four men who floated leisurely down the placid waters of Glen Canyon, perhaps the most eventful part of the trip occurred at their destination, for at the mouth of the Paria they met the mysterious John D. Lee.

John D. Lee was an important figure in early-day southern Utah. As noted earlier, Lee was one of the select group to accompany Brigham Young, Major Powell, and Jacob Hamblin to the banks of the upper Paria River in 1870. During that trip, Lee noted in his diary that Brigham Young had asked him if he would like to establish a mission on the Paria. Appalled by the suggestion, Lee recorded his reply: "I would want no greater punishment than to be Sent on a Mission to the Pahariere. I would turn out Indian at once & take no woman to such a place."[9]

Powell's men little realized how ironic it was to find Lee, in 1872, living on the banks of the Paria. Moreover, on the Lee's Ferry Ranch now lived one of Lee's wives, Emma, and their children. Lee *had* taken a woman to such a place.

John D. Lee, scapegoat for the Mountain Meadows Massacre and founder of Lee's Ferry, was photographed about 1860. *Courtesy Utah State Historical Society*

6 THE LEE OF LEE'S FERRY

If the matter were judged dispassionately, perhaps Lee's Ferry should not have been so named. It was Jacob Hamblin who used the crossing first, and it was his interest and initiative that led to the establishment of the ferry by the Church of Jesus Christ of Latter-day Saints. When service was actually started, John D. Lee was on hand only long enough to convey a few travelers across the river. Nevertheless, Lee was the first operator and the first settler. Furthermore, his commanding personality and his notoriety insured the perpetuation of his name.

John Doyle Lee, one of the leading colonizers of southern Utah, helped establish the towns of Parowan and Harmony. Later he pioneered further south into Utah's "Dixie," in the present St. George area. A man of wide abilities, Lee served variously as farmer, miller, judge, legislator, tavern keeper, and ferryman. In earlier years he had worked as a clerk for Brigham Young. On many occasions the Mormon leader expressed or demonstrated his affection for Lee, even calling Lee his "adopted" son.[1]

In religious matters Lee often revealed a touch of the fanatic. He was quick to voice righteous indignation at those Mormons whose conduct was tinged with human weakness. To Lee, what the Church or Brigham Young said was law, regardless of conflict with secular statutes. Given the example by high Church leaders, Lee zealously embraced the doctrine of polygamy, eventually marrying nineteen women.

Lee's inflexibility and intolerance toward wayward Mormons left him unpopular among his own people. Yet he commanded respect. He was aggressive and industrious, and when a difficult job had to be done, Lee was often given the assignment.

Lee's trail to Lee's Ferry was a long one, covering a full fourteen years of his life. It all hinged on the Mountain Meadows Massacre back in 1857 and on the role Lee played in that tragedy.

To be understood, the Mountain Meadows Massacre must be put into the context of the times. In 1847 and 1848, thousands of Mormons moved west to free themselves from harassment and persecution at the hands of punitive neighbors in Missouri and Illinois. Once settled in Utah the Saints labored hard to gain sustenance, if not prosperity, from the recent wilderness.

But as the Great Basin commonwealth of Mormons grew and seemed to thrive, their relations with federal authorities gradually deteriorated. Tension mounted to critical pitch when, in 1857, the federal government sent a military force of 2500 men under Colonel Albert Sidney Johnston to depose Brigham Young as territorial governor, put down any armed resistance, and enforce federal authority. As the army approached, excitement and emotion among the Saints ran high. Excesses of rhetorical invective inflamed mob passions, leading to actual preparations for war. If anything, unchecked emotionalism was more intense in the outlying settlements where slow communication compounded rumor and fact, creating an atmosphere of hysterical uncertainty.[2]

Into this explosive atmosphere, in the late summer days of 1857, came the Fancher Train, an emigrant group of about a hundred and forty men, women, and children. Most of them were from Arkansas. After leaving Salt Lake City, the emigrants headed south over the all-weather route to southern California.

Apparently the Fancher Train encountered trouble soon after leaving the Utah capital city. Mormons along the way refused to sell them provisions. The emigrants countered with abusive language; some of them boasted of having helped to drive the Mormons out of Missouri. Cattle were turned into fields, and some Mormons claimed that water supplies were intentionally fouled. Name calling was freely indulged in by both sides. The situation worsened as the train moved south. To local Mormons caught up in the hysteria provoked by the ominous approach of Johnston's army, the emigrants appeared to symbolize all injustices the Saints had suffered, past and present.

At this point, the local Paiute Indians became involved. The Paiutes and the Mormons had agreed to act as allies if war broke out with the federal government. Observing Mormon belligerence toward the Fancher Train, the Paiutes became eager to launch an attack on the "enemy." In the past, Indians living along main-traveled roads had suffered from the thoughtlessness of passing emigrants, who often shot the natives on the slightest pretext, or none at all. Now the tribesmen would have a chance to get even.

In the southwest corner of present-day Utah, at the edge of the long desert road ahead, the Fancher party camped for several days in a green valley while their stock gained strength. Local settlers knew this green valley as Mountain Meadows. At Cedar City, about twenty miles east of Mountain Meadows, Mormon leaders resolved that the Fancher Train should not be allowed to escape. But because the actual killing might be distasteful, they decided to turn the job over to their Paiute Indian "allies." Since Jacob Hamblin, the regular Indian sub-agent, was in northern Utah at the time, the L.D.S. stake president sent for John D. Lee, the so-called Indian Farmer, to "manage the Indians."

Lee objected to the job but felt that he could not refuse. Not only was the stake president Lee's religious superior; he was also Lee's military superior in the Nauvoo Legion, the Mormon militia.

Given Mormon acquiescence, the Paiutes eagerly rode down upon the emigrants, even before John D. Lee could arrive on the scene. Although startled by the attack the emigrants rallied quickly and were soon returning a deadly fire that inflicted losses on the Indians. The Paiutes retreated, but kept the wagon train under seige.

Now the Indians felt betrayed; neither the Mormon God nor their Mormon allies had protected them. When Lee did arrive he was told by the Paiutes that if the Mormons did not assist in another attack, the Indians might make war on the Mormons themselves. Educated guesses date the tragedy on or about September 11, 1857, early in the morning.

On Christmas Day, 1871, John D. Lee inscribed his name on the cliff above House Rock Spring, located about a day's ride northwest of Lee's Ferry.

On the Lee's Ferry Ranch, also known as Lonely Dell, stand two log buildings reportedly built by John D. Lee.

28

About fifty Mormon men rode toward the emigrant train, but stopped some distance away while John D. Lee and a man named William Bateman rode on, under a flag of truce. Lee and Bateman proposed that the emigrants surrender their arms, that they give their cattle to the Indians, and that the accused among them be taken to Mormon jails to be held for misdemeanor trials. Although the offer was not a good one, the emigrants felt that it was the only way to escape with their lives. They accepted.

The waiting Mormons then rode into camp, gathered the arms, sent the women and older children on ahead, and put the younger children in a wagon. A Mormon walked beside each male emigrant until all were in line. Major John Higbee then crested the hill and shouted the order, "Do Your Duty!"

Upon this command each Mormon turned and killed the emigrant next to him. A few hundred yards ahead, the women and children turned at the sound of gunfire only to see hundreds of Indians rushing at them from the tall bushes. Within a few minutes all emigrants were dead, excepting only eighteen small children who had been taken by wagon over a nearby hill. Years later Lee stated that he tried to "do his duty," but that his gun fired prematurely, slightly wounding a fellow Mormon.

So ended the Mountain Meadow Massacre—a field of blood-spattered brush and grass, still-warm bodies in death's posture, a band of Indians systematically rifling corpses, eighteen frightened children crying for their parents, Mormon men suddenly aghast and revolted by the horrible scene.[3]

During the 1850s, even though industry and hard work were commonplace, communications and the pace of life in remote southern Utah were quite slow. Months, even years, went by before much was generally known about the massacre. Rumors that such an atrocity had indeed occurred were confirmed by a visit to the site by a U.S. Army detachment in May 1859. The soldiers buried a few scattered bones and put up a stone cairn, but they learned almost nothing about why or how the massacre took place. The over fifty Mormon men who had participated remained not only free but largely unsuspected by those outside the southern Utah villages. Even before the army visit to the site, the president of the Southern Utah Mission, George A. Smith, realized that outsiders would eventually learn much of the truth, and he hoped to keep blame from being attached either to Brigham Young or to the LDS Church as a whole. Smith therefore held a number of public hearings to obtain facts on the massacre.

In August 1858, after one of the hearings in Parowan—one that John D. Lee did not attend—a report was issued stating, "It is reported that John D. Lee and a few other white men were on the ground during a portion of the combat." From this first accusation, however tentative,

Emma Batchelder Lee, seventeenth wife of John D. Lee, was the first woman to live at Lee's Ferry. She was known for her stamina and firm character. *Courtesy Utah State Historical Society*

can be traced Lee's growing role as scapegoat, resulting in his eventual banishment to the Colorado River as well as his final personal tragedy.

Lee had a few more years of comparative freedom from worry, for although he had been named as a participant and although a warrant for his arrest had been issued, no Mormon would reveal Lee's whereabouts. Nevertheless, pressure on the Church continued to mount; Church leaders were accused of harboring a fugitive, if not of outright complicity in the crime.

In late 1870, just after his trip to the upper Paria with Brigham Young and Major Powell, the Church officially excommunicated Lee for his part in the massacre. In his diary Lee recorded that he rode to St. George where he told Brigham Young that "I suffered the blame to rest on Me, when it should rest on Persons whoes Names that have never been brought out & that if any Man had told to the contrary, his informant had lied like Hell." In spite of his protest, however, no formal hearing on his excommunication was held. Instead he was sent an anonymous letter stating, "Trust no one. Make yourself scarce & keep out of the way."[4]

At the semi-annual Church conference held at St. George in the fall of 1871, Lee's future was apparently discussed. Almost certainly, Jacob Hamblin was the one who suggested that Lee be sent to the mouth of the Paria to establish a ferry crossing of the Colorado River. Brigham Young accepted the suggestion and sent the order to Lee.

On December 4, 1871, Lee, with one of his sons and two other men, took fifty-seven head of cattle and left the village of Pahreah (now spelled Paria), heading south toward the Colorado River. Incredibly, they traveled right down the forty-mile long, narrow, twisting, canyon floor of the Paria River. Lee's diary comment sums up the ordeal.

We concluded to drive down the creek, which took us Some 8 days of toil, fatuige, & labour, through brush, water, ice, & quicksand & some time passing through narrow chasms with perpendicular Bluffs on both sides, some 3000 feet high, & without seeing the sun for 48 hours, & every day Some of our animals Mired down & had to shoot one cow & leve her there, that we count not get out, & I My Self was under water, Mud & Ice every day....My Son & My self also carried 1 & ½ Bus. seed corn with us from the Setlement & it was Baptised as often as I was & one place it was under water 24 hours before I could find it, & had pased the place some 10 miles. Finally returned & found it.[5]

Lee reached the Colorado River on December 12, finding the place deserted. Major Powell's men had just left to spend the winter in Kanab. Upset that many members of his family, traveling by wagon, had not arrived, Lee set out on the "supposed wagon road" to find them. But there was no road; no wagons had ever yet been taken across the Kaibab and through House Rock Valley to the mouth of the Paria. While searching for the "road" Lee and his son wandered into a region of rough gulches, taking five days to reach his wife Emma's house several miles northeast of Kanab.

After resting a few days, Lee and Emma loaded a wagon and headed for the mouth of the Paria. This time Lee made the Kaibab crossing at a better spot, passed House Rock Spring (where, on Christmas Day, he carved his name in the sandstone), and reached his destination without serious trouble.

By this time Lee's other family members—those Lee had searched for earlier—were there to greet him. Principal among them were Lee's wife Rachel, a few older children, and several younger children.

The next day Emma obtained her first real look at the barren cliffs that rose in profusion about her new home. Sensing the brooding isolation that separated her family from even the smallest settlement, she cried, "Oh, what a lonely dell." Struck by her remark, Lee decided that the name for the place should be Lonely Dell.[6]

For the rest of his life, Lee and his family always referred to the place as Lonely Dell. But to the world it was a hideout where the infamous John D. Lee lived and worked. It was Lee's Ferry.

The dawn of a new year, 1872, found Lee and his sons building stone and wooden shelters for his families. For the first time Lee's Ferry had residents who intended to stay.

7 FORGING THE VITAL LINK

During his first year at Lee's Ferry, Lee spent little time taking people across the river. In the first place he didn't have a ferryboat. What crossings he did make were more in the character of memorable incidents than routine business.

In January 1872, Lee obtained his first customers—a band of fifteen Navajos heading north to trade. For a makeshift ferryboat Lee found, near the river bank, the flat-bottomed scow *Cañon Maid,* that Powell and Hamblin had used to cross the river in 1870. By caulking it, Lee made the craft serviceable enough to carry the Navajos across.[1]

But the *Cañon Maid* did not serve long as a ferryboat. One day in April, while Lee was on his cattle range in House Rock Valley, a prospector named Parker and his men rode up to tell Lee what had happened to the *Cañon Maid.*

Parker and his fellow prospectors were apparently in the van of the first gold rush to reach these Colorado River canyons. Hearing that gold had been found in the river sands and nearby gravel bars, several groups of prospectors had set out for the few places where they could reach the river—including Lee's Ferry.

Lee had met Parker at Lee's Ferry in March, and since Parker carried letters of reference from leading Mormons, Lee knew that Parker would not expose him as a fugitive. Although they worked the river thoroughly at the mouth of the Paria, the prospectors could find only traces of gold, not the rich bars that they believed lay beside the river further downstream.

Parker's story to Lee was that the prospectors, wishing to investigate possible gold deposits downriver, took the *Cañon Maid* and floated down into Marble Canyon! They also took along a crude raft to carry supplies. Apparently they reached Badger Creek Rapids and possibly Soap Creek Rapids when both the *Cañon Maid* and the raft were smashed against rocks and destroyed. Somehow all the men escaped with their lives, though they lost their gear and some of Lee's tools.[2]

A few days later seven Navajos, returning from a trading trip to Kanab, showed up at Lee's Ferry and asked Lee to take them across the Colorado. Lee told them he had no boat but the Indians had seen the *Nellie Powell,* one of Powell's three boats that had been cached in 1871. These Navajos insisted that Lee take them over in this boat. Lee finally agreed, but with the stipulation that the Navajos first work on the dam and irrigation ditch until water flowed to his ranch house. This they did, but their help turned out to be worse than none, for they were lazy, they frequently stole potatoes and other food, and in general they were, in Lee's words, a "Band of low Maraders from the chief down." When the time for river crossing arrived, Lee had to buckle on a revolver in order to back up his commands. The incident ended with the Navajos and Lee shouting insults to each other as the latter rowed back across the river.[3]

Lee used the *Nellie Powell* once more during 1872 when he conveyed Powell's former photographer, E. O. Beaman, across the river in August.[4]

While Lee was plowing a field at the Lee's Ferry Ranch, the four Powell men who, having retrieved their cached boat, had just floated through Glen Canyon, arrived on July 13. A few days later the group that had traveled overland from the mouth of the Dirty Devil also arrived. The meeting of these men with John D. Lee was no surprise to either party, since both had knowledge of each other's activities.

The youthful boatmen could even find humor in Lee's status as a fugitive from justice. Dellenbaugh, relating a story about Andy Hattan, the cook, and Lee, says that,

> Brother Lee...called to give us a lengthy dissertation on the faith of the Latter-day Saints (Mormons), while Andy, always up

to mischief, in his quiet way, delighted to get behind him and cock a rifle. At the sound of the ominous click Lee would wheel like a flash to see what was up. We had no intention of capturing him, of course, but it amused Andy to act in a way that kept Lee on the *qui vive.*[5]

Major Powell did not arrive for the voyage through the Grand Canyon for another month, so the men with little to do helped Lee on the grueling task of putting in an irrigation system. In return, Lee and Emma frequently had the "boys" over for dinner.

Major Powell's arrival on August 13 was the occasion for the second meeting between Powell and Lee, the first having occurred on the trip to the upper Paria valley in 1870. Lee greeted Powell as an old friend.

On August 17, after Emma had served breakfast to the entire crew, Powell and his men departed for their voyage through the Grand Canyon—actually the second leg of Powell's second trip. For three weeks during 1872 Powell and his six men fought rocks and unwieldly boats until, at the mouth of Kanab Creek, the Major called it quits. Although a supply train was on hand to meet him, he decided to abandon the boats and leave the river.

John D. Lee and Major Powell never met again. Whereas Lee had not long to live, Powell went on to become a giant in governmental science programs. In later years the Major headed his own independent land survey, the U.S. Geological Survey, the Irrigation Survey, and the Bureau of American Ethnology. And his persuasive influence helped to create the Bureau of Reclamation.

In the fall of 1872, lumber sent by the Mormon Church for the first real ferryboat arrived at Lee's Ferry. Brigham Young and other leading Mormons had long considered Arizona within their territory. Years before, Arizona had been included in the projections for the huge State of Deseret that was proclaimed by Young but largely ignored by Congress. Jacob Hamblin's missionary efforts to the Hopis were not totally religious in nature; he was also assessing prospects for Mormon settlements.

Hamblin's unfavorable early reports on Indian hostilities and on the rugged nature of northern Arizona held up colonization efforts until the southern Utah towns were free of Indian wars and strong enough to support more remote settlements. By 1872 the potential looked good enough in the Little Colorado Valley to organize a colonizing expedition. To travel to the south, however, colonists would have to cross the Colorado River and would require a sturdy ferryboat at Lee's Ferry. The ferry was indeed regarded as a vital link in plans to extend the Mormon frontier into Arizona Territory.

Built largely by a crew of Mormons sent from St. George, the first ferryboat was launched on January 11, 1873. It was 26 feet long and 8½

The first major expedition to colonize in Arizona found no "suitable" land and so returned to Utah. As attested by this inscription at House Rock Spring, they "busted."

feet wide and was named by Lee *Colorado*. A small skiff named the *Pahreah* was also launched.[6]

Within a few days a Mormon exploring expedition led by Lorenzo W. Roundy and Jacob Hamblin arrived and was taken across the river in the new ferryboat. The trip took Roundy and Hamblin and their men south to the San Francisco Peaks and east through part of the Little Colorado River Valley, which they declared on their return was suitable for settlement. Church authorities thereupon put out a "call," instructing selected men and their families to move to Arizona.[7]

While awaiting the colonists, Hamblin and Lee argued about the actual placement of the ferry crossing. Jacob noted correctly that if the crossing were made below the Paria, it would take only a short dugway to reach the general level of the valley floor, the Marble Platform. Lee pointed out, however, that the south side river bank was practically a sheer cliff, and the narrow rock landing would be submerged during periods of high water. Furthermore, a crossing right at the head of

Rachel Woolsey Lee, sixth wife of John D. Lee, was steadfastly loyal to her husband throughout his ordeals. *Courtesy Utah State Historical Society*

Marble Canyon might place the ferryboat and its passengers in danger. Lee wrote in his diary, "I would expect to hear of the Boats being caried away & Some Persons drownded."[8]

A far safer crossing, Lee said, could be made about one-half mile above the Paria, below the big bend in the river. The biggest drawback to this site would be expense since longer and more costly approach roads would be necessary, particularly on the south side. Once across the river travelers would be forced to ascend the steep rough ledge of Shinarump Conglomerate later referred to disparagingly as "Lee's Backbone" (see Tour Site No. 13).

Stake President Joseph W. Young and Bishop Edward Bunker, after inspecting the sites, agreed that safety was paramount; the ferry would cross the river at Lee's preferred site.

In May 1873, the colonists began arriving. About seventy wagons with emigrant families, plus their horses and cattle, were in the three separate contingents. Horton Haight was the overall commander of the wagon train. After the first two groups of about fifty wagons had been taken across the river, the river rose and became more swift, forcing Lee to move the *Colorado* further upstream, around the bend.

Since no approach roads had been built to reach this revised site, it was difficult for travelers to get their wagons to and from the ferryboat. Henry Day, the leader of the third contingent, complained angrily to Lee that "it was a Poor Shitten arrangemt & that this compay never Should have been Sent on a Mission until a good Road & Ferry had been Made first." Lee replied sharply, giving Day a stern lecture on the duties of a pioneer. According to Lee's diary, this seemed to silence Mr. Day.[9]

Other emigrants at Lee's Ferry that day seemed to take a different

Rachel Lee's first desert home was a shanty at Jacob's Pools, a desolate spot at the base of the Vermilion Cliffs. *Courtesy Utah State Historical Society*

view of John D. Lee. Andrew Amundsen, a Norwegian missionary who used inimitable spelling, wrote in his journal:

> when we got ther we found John DeLee working at the boat and two others. efter dinner we crosed ouer animalls and one Wagon. Dealee wass very jocky, and jovele, full of fun…The Morning wass very calm no wind, and the Rivver still, the Wether pretty and clear, birds singing and all injoyed a good spirrit. we then comenst crosing ouer Wagons, all over sef and sound.[10]

The colonists did not stay long in Arizona Territory. In early June 1873, the sound of gunfire brought Lee to the river bank where he saw two of the Arizona colonizers. They reported to Lee that the large expedition had "busted" and that they were returning to Utah. "Nothing but sand and rock, and crooked cottonwoods" in the Little Colorado Valley, they told Lee. Disgusted at their lack of faith and persistence, Lee nevertheless ferried the two travelers back across the river.

Before the main expedition arrived, however, a violent thunderstorm toppled a large cottonwood into the mooring of the ferryboat. By the time Lee got to the scene, the *Colorado* had broken loose and had disappeared into the depths of Marble Canyon. When the would-be settlers arrived at the south bank, Lee was able to convey them across in the small skiff, the *Pahreah*. No mention is made of the disposition of the wagons.

As useful as he was in his new role as ferryman, John D. Lee was still a fugitive. When told the rumor (unfounded, as it turned out), that troops from Camp Douglas in Utah were on their way to Lee's Ferry to set up a military post, Lee had no choice but to flee. Following the route of the recent emigrant train, he headed south, further into Arizona, following the Echo Cliffs. On the cliffside about sixty miles from Lee's Ferry he found a good spring, called by the Hopis "Moenave," where he set up a small ranch.

Jacob Hamblin had already made a claim on this spring at Moenave so Lee made a trade with him. In return for Lee's outpost ranch in House Rock Valley called Jacob Pools, Hamblin turned over the Moenave property to Lee. Lee's wife Rachel, who had been living at Jacob Pools, then moved to Moenave.

Lee spent the last five months of 1873 at Moenave. During that time his wife Emma carried on at Lee's Ferry with her small children. In November she gave birth to another child, without benefit of a midwife, nurse, or doctor. Appropriately, Emma named her daughter Victoria in memory of her personal victory over isolation and hardship. Three days after this blessed event, Lee arrived.

Late in 1873 Mormon workmen from the St. George Stake again journeyed to Lee's Ferry to build a ferryboat. Its immediate purpose was to convey a new colonizing expedition across the river in 1874.[11]

8 LEE'S FERRY FORT

Of the present buildings at Lee's Ferry, only one stands out as an obvious relic of the past. A small structure of rough-cut, random-sized rocks holding a thatched roof of sticks, willows, and mud, it blends into the landscape and holds its secrets in mute decay. Referred to as Lee's Ferry Fort (or erroneously as Lee's Fort), its thick walls and narrow windows imply that violence, or the threat of it, was once reality itself along this river of the West.

Yet the fort is not so much a monument to violence as to frustration, for the building symbolizes the year 1874, when Mormon plans to colonize northern Arizona were blocked by the malevolence and misdeeds of other men.

It was early January, 1874. A hundred miles north of Lee's Ferry, four young Navajo men rode south on their return from a trading trip to the Ute country. On their way they passed into Grass Valley, which had just been settled by Mormons and a few "Gentiles" the previous year. At one of the ranch houses they stopped, probably in hopes of obtaining food.

Apparently entering without knocking, they found William McCarty and his sons cooking breakfast. A visitor named Clinger was also in the kitchen. The Navajos, although ordered to leave, placed themselves between the white men and the guns stacked in a corner. The Indians then forced McCarty, his sons, and Clinger to leave, but the settlers took refuge in the barn—while the Navajos ate the breakfast in the house.

McCarty and Clinger then realized that the guns in the house were useless to the Navajos, since all available ammunition was in the gun belts the white men still wore. Devising a plan, the McCarty boys gathered some hay, tied it into a bundle, and began rolling it toward the house, perhaps preparatory to setting it on fire. Seeing this, the Navajos panicked and ran. Two of them jumped on Clinger's horse, while the other two took their own horses.

Immediately, the white settlers obtained their guns from the house and opened fire. The two Indians on their own horses were killed, but those on Clinger's horse rode out of sight. Within a few minutes the McCartys saddled up and gave chase. When they finally caught the Navajos they killed one of them, wounded the other, and shot Clinger's horse. The wounded Navajo escaped into a rough canyon and hid out until oncoming darkness finally forced the McCartys to give up the search and return home.[1]

The wounded Navajo, Ne-Chic-Se-Cla, then began his long walk south. Somehow the youthful Indian covered the distance, crossed the river at Crossing of the Fathers, and reached his home near Moenkopi. Upon hearing his version of the story, the Navajo leaders were outraged, many of them even suggesting all-out war on southern Utah settlers. Two of the Navajos killed were sons of a leading chief in the tribe.[2]

Unimportant to the Navajos but a vital point to the Mormons was the fact that William McCarty was not a Mormon. McCarty and his sons, Tom, Bill, and George, had just moved to the area. In later years, Tom and Bill became notorious western outlaws, associating with a group known loosely as the Wild Bunch. They were often led by another man from southern Utah, Robert LeRoy Parker, also known as Butch Cassidy.

While many Navajos were calling for bloody revenge, a Hopi chief named Tuba who had befriended whites in the past learned of the Indian war council and rushed to the nearest white settler, who happened to be John D. Lee. Lee was on another of his periodic departures from Lee's Ferry and was working on his new ranch at Moenave. Told of the imminent Indian War, Lee immediately saddled up and rode north to Lee's Ferry on a cold and foggy night. When he reached the ferry the next day his sons carried the message on to the town of Pahreah, and then to Jacob Hamblin at Kanab.

About a week later, Lee was out on his cattle range in House Rock Valley when he met Jacob Hamblin heading for the ferry. Hamblin, acting on telegraphed instructions from Brigham Young, was on his way to meet with the Navajo chiefs and, hopefully, to prevent a war. Lee returned with Hamblin as far as Moenave where he found his ranch house converted into a virtual fortress, complete with sand bags and rifle ports.[3]

About February 1, 1874, Hamblin did meet with the chiefs in a grueling twelve-hour session where he was accused of lying and deceiving the Indians. Tension within the large hogan was so intense at times that Hamblin thought he would be killed. At last the Indian leaders allowed Hamblin to leave, but only after he promised to seek reparations in the form of cattle and other stock and to meet again with the Navajos in twenty-five days.[4]

But Hamblin did not keep his word. He knew that the struggling settlements of southern Utah could not afford to send hundreds of cattle and horses as reparations. Furthermore, he felt that the Mormons were not to blame. That he failed to keep his appointment with the Navajos only increased the Indians' irritation and anger.

40

Into this explosive atmosphere John Blythe led a small company of Mormon colonists south from Lee's Ferry toward Moenkopi. Lee himself was on hand to ferry them across the river. Although the Mormons reached Moenkopi without incident, they were soon harrassed by Navajos, who rode wildly through the village each day yelling and taunting the settlers.

Since Hamblin had failed to keep his appointment with the chiefs, the Navajos demanded that Blythe and Ira Hatch come to their council hogan and "talk things over." Reluctantly Blythe and Hatch complied, only to find themselves virtually on trial, with their lives in balance. Many hours later it was finally decided to release Hatch and to burn Blythe at the stake. Blythe's steadfast refusal to show fear, however, turned the odds in his favor, and both men were released.

When word reached Kanab that missionaries to Moenkopi were being held hostage, a rescue force of fifty men was organized under John R. Young. This group crossed at Lee's Ferry and rushed south in time to prevent an expected attack on Moenkopi.[5] For the time being, however, the mission to Moenkopi was finished. Settlers could not live peacefully in the midst of a hostile Indian land, nor could they garrison a village adequately for defense. Their only choice was to return to Utah Territory.

In May 1874, Hamblin and other Mormons sent a letter to all Navajo chiefs that included the following:

If a few of your good men will come over the Colorado, with a good Spanish interpreter, we will meet you at our Ferry Boat, where we will be happy to see you, and satisfy you that what we have said is true. But should any attempt to cross the Colorado above our Ferry Boat we shall look upon them as enemies.[6]

In other words, Lee's Ferry was to be the only point of friendly Navajo-Mormon contact.

Anticipating that the Navajos would come to Lee's Ferry to negotiate, Hamblin was anxious to make the place important to them, not only as a place to talk but as a place of trade. At the May semi-annual Mormon conference, held in 1874 at St. George, Jacob therefore proposed that a trading post be built at Lee's Ferry. A useful trading post would mean that Navajos would not have to journey into the Utah settlements to trade, which would be easier for the Indians and considerably safer for the Mormon villages. Brigham Young agreed to the suggestion and ordered construction of the post.

In June 1874, a group of at least fifteen men, led by Andrew Gibbon and Thales Haskell, began work on the building "a little above the Lee Ferry on the Colorado."[7] Although called a trading post, it was also referred to as a fortification, giving it a dual purpose. By July the small rock structure was finished, ready for the Navajos. But the attitude of

Lee's Ferry Fort is inspected by some of Charles H. Spencer's mining men in 1910. Spencer later built an addition onto the west end and converted the fort into a cook house for his men. *Courtesy A. H. Jones, Elizabeth, Colorado*

the Navajos continued hostile, keeping them from any peaceful contact with Mormons.

The Grass Valley affair was simply another in a series of Navajo grievances against whites in general and against the Indian Bureau in particular. Agent W.F.M. Arny at Fort Defiance sided strongly against the Mormons, blaming them for the Grass Valley killings, but the reasons for his hasty accusation seem unclear. The matter was, however, one of the subjects he proposed to discuss with administration leaders when he escorted a group of Navajo chiefs to Washington. In September 1874, Arny and the traveling chiefs met with President Grant, but what they discussed was not recorded. If Grass Valley came up at all, the President did nothing about the matter.[8]

So few of the Navajo demands were acceded to by government officials that the tribesmen considered the Washington trip to have been virtually a waste of time and money. They placed blame on Agent W.F.M. Arny, which helped contribute to his early dismissal from the post. In this way Arny became the scapegoat for many Navajo dissatisfactions—including the Grass Valley killings—indirectly bringing peace to the Mormon-Indian borderlands.

Of some value also was the inspection trip—at Jacob Hamblin's urging—of Navajo Chief Hastele to the Grass Valley area. Hamblin reported that Hastele was satisfied that Mormons were not involved in the killings. In a late summer conference at Fort Defiance, Hamblin and Hastele spoke to a group of tribal leaders. According to Hamblin, "The truth was brought to light, and those who wished to throw the blame of murdering the young Navajos upon the Saints were confounded."

The small trading post now called Lee's Ferry Fort thus began operations, although how much business it handled is not known. Jacob himself worked as a part-time trader during the winter of 1874-75. Other Mormons also served as traders during the next two or three years. It is doubtful that the post continued operations into the 1880s.

In 1910 a miner-promoter named Charles H. Spencer who planned a big operation at Lee's Ferry added a wing onto the west end of the old fort and converted the whole structure into a mess hall. But by 1913 the miners had departed. Spencer's additional wing was later either partially torn down or gradually collapsed. (For more details of Spencer's operations, see Chapter 12.) The original 1874 fort remains virtually intact (see Tour Site No. 4).

Although John D. Lee, by carrying the first warning of Navajo unrest from Moenave to Lee's Ferry, became involved in the Mormon Navajo disputes of 1874, he apparently played no further role. He continued to operate the ferry from time to time and to farm at both Lee's Ferry and Moenave. He made at least one trip with some prospectors to the San Francisco Mountain region of Arizona. While on this trip he met some friendly Havasupai Indians, who may have invited him to visit their canyon village. Since Lee's diary for most of 1874 is missing, it can only be said that he spent little time at Lee's Ferry. According to certain stories he spent considerable time visiting the Indians in Havasu Canyon. Perhaps the stories are true.[9]

In November 1874, Sheriff William Stokes of Beaver, Utah, acting on the still valid warrant for Lee's arrest, heard that Lee was somewhere in the Utah settlements. After receiving more reports, Stokes concluded that Lee must be at Panguitch, perhaps visiting his wife Caroline. Upon reaching Caroline's house and questioning Lee's family, Stokes guessed that Lee must be hiding in the chicken coop that was covered with straw. Peering through a hole in the straw, Stokes saw Lee holding a Smith and Wesson five shooter. Several times Lee was ordered out by Stokes and his four deputies until Stokes said, "If he makes a single move, I'll blow his brains out!" Lee quickly replied, "Hold on boys. Don't get excited. I'll come out."[10]

Thus on November 7, 1874, Lee was captured and taken to the jail in Beaver to await trial. At the trial, which began in July 1875, many details of the Mountain Meadows Massacre were aired, but little evidence pointed to Lee's guilt. It appeared indeed that Lee had played at most only a minor role. Yet the jury was split, with the eight Mormons being for acquittal and the four Gentiles for conviction. Another trial would be required.[11]

When Lee was released on bail in May 1876, he rode south from Beaver—a man growing embittered at the scapegoat role he saw being forced upon him. Still he clung to the frail belief that the Mormon presidency, as well as other leaders, would speak in his behalf and that he would be acquitted. Until his second trial, which was set for September,

43

At Mountain Meadows, March 23, 1877, John D. Lee sits on his coffin awaiting execution by a firing squad. At his left the Deputy U.S. Marshal reads the death warrant. On horseback in the background are Lee's sons. They were kept at a distance as it was feared they would attempt a last minute rescue of their father. The firing squad is hidden under the wagon canvas at far right. *Courtesy Library of Congress*

he could visit those few friends that continued to stand by him. Although his diary for the period is missing, he evidently divided his time among his wives and families, going to Lee's Ferry, Skutumpah, Panguitch, and Moenave.

When urged to jump bail and to take refuge in Mexico, Lee refused. After he had left on his return to the Beaver jail, a messenger reportedly arrived at Lee's Ferry with advice from the Church authorities suggesting that Lee should leave the country. The Church would assume responsibility for the bail bond. But the messenger missed Lee, and Lee was back in jail before he received a report about the messenger.

At the second trial, the tone had changed. Appealing to emotions, the prosecution presented hearsay evidence, innuendos, and apparent contradictions. Jacob Hamblin who was in northern Utah at the time of the massacre, even testified against Lee. Yet Lee presented no defense. If he was relying on the all-Mormon jury to acquit him he was mistaken, for he was found guilty and was sentenced to be shot by a firing squad. Although the territorial governor offered to commute Lee's sentence if he would make a full confession, Lee refused.

On the morning of March 23, 1877, Lee was taken to Mountain Meadows, where a firing squad and a coffin awaited him. Before being blindfolded, he stated, "I am ready to die. I trust in God. I have no fear. Death has no terror." The sound of five shots signaled the death of John Doyle Lee.

For the next seventy-three years the Mormon Church maintained that Lee was solely responsible for the massacre. Then in 1950 a courageous Mormon lady named Juanita Brooks published a book, *The Mountain Meadows Massacre,* that detailed the true story. In 1961 Church authorities reinstated Lee to membership in the Church. A special marker was placed on his grave, reading:

"Ye Shall Know the Truth,
And the Truth Shall Make You Free."
John 8:32

44

9 ON TO ARIZONA

Long before Lee was actually captured, Mormon Church authorities realized that Lee's Ferry, the vital link between Mormon settlements in Utah and Arizona, should not be controlled by a fugitive who spent much of his time in hiding. In December 1872, a young man named James Jackson was sent to help, but Jackson's weak physique and inexperience were ill-suited to the demands of the assignment. Apparently about the only thing Jackson could do was teach school for Lee's children. Jackson lived in a small cabin on ten acres of sandy soil along the Paria just north of Lee's ranch. On March 10, 1874, Jackson died from exposure and poor general health while out on the Kaibab Plateau.[1] Although his was the first burial in the Lee's Ferry Cemetery, his grave is marked only by a collection of loose stones (see Tour Site No. 9).

Another man, stronger, more mature, and proven in wilderness trials was needed. The man picked for the job was Warren M. Johnson, then a school teacher in Glendale, Utah, but a man who had served well on the rugged pioneering mission to the Muddy River, Nevada. A Mormon convert, Johnson was devout, sincere, hard-working, and dependable—just the type of man needed for the job.[2]

After receiving the "call" in October 1873, Johnson moved the older of his two wives, Permelia, to Lee's Ferry in March 1875. Since Emma Lee was still living at the ranch house, Johnson moved into the cabin vacated the year before by James Jackson. Johnson finally moved his younger wife, Samantha, to the river early in 1876. Samantha and her young child were housed in the trading post, Lee's Ferry Fort. Later he moved both families into the fort.

Failure of the Haight mission in 1873 had been compounded by the Indian unrest of 1874, but Church leaders persisted in their efforts to colonize Arizona Territory. A scouting expedition headed by James S. Brown crossed the ferry and headed south in 1875, traveling up the valley of the Little Colorado. Brown's favorable report again set serious colonizing in motion, with about two hundred missionaries "called" from many parts of Utah.

The first settlers crossed the river without mishap and arrived at their destination on the Little Colorado March 23, 1876, but the migration continued for many weeks thereafter.

As the widow of John D. Lee, Emma Lee continued to have a proprietary interest in the ferry. In this connection, Warren Johnson would

Warren Marshall Johnson (center) operated Lee's Ferry and the ranch from 1875 to 1896. He is shown with his wife, Permelia (left), and some of his children. In the doorway holding the baby is Vina Brinkerhoff, wife of Johnson's assistant David Brinkerhoff. *Courtesy Frank Johnson, St. George, Utah*

have been Emma's employee, but what financial arrangements they had are unknown. Some emigrant diary accounts suggest that Emma, at least on occasion, actually rowed the ferryboat herself. Indeed she was said to be quite competent.

Emma Lee, however, had little reason to remain at this isolated and remote river crossing. In May 1879, the Mormon Church bought the ferry rights from her for $3,000, paid mostly in cattle.[3] She then moved south, farther into Arizona, where she married again and lived until 1897.

The successful colonizing expedition of 1876 led to larger and more ambitious emigrations in following years. From 1876 to about 1890, use of Lee's Ferry was most intensive, for it served as the critical river crossing for many hundreds of Mormons heading into Arizona.

In spite of boating safety precautions, the river remained an ever-present danger, especially when the ferry was operated by inexperienced persons. On May 28, 1876, Daniel H. Wells, counselor to the L.D.S. president, showed up at the river with Erastus Snow, Jacob Hamblin,

Bishop Lorenzo Roundy, and other high-placed Mormons, all on their way to Arizona. After loading the wagons and passengers, Warren Johnson ordered the boat towed upstream along the bank to the crossing point. Probably he should have had two lines on the boat rather than one. While the boat was being maneuvered around a point of rock the single tow line caught on a rock, causing the boat to dip into the current. Everyone and everything on board were thrown into the river.

Hamblin reported that he and some others managed to reach shore, launch a skiff, and save the wagons and most of the other people. Lorenzo W. Roundy, however, never surfaced. Either he was struck by the boat or he suffered a cramp and drowned. The ferryboat went on down the river into Marble Canyon and was never seen again. The party finally completed its river crossing by carrying its disassembled wagons over in the skiff.[4]

During these early years, if passengers were lucky enough to escape the river unharmed they still faced the terrible piece of road known as Lee's Backbone, a one and one-half-mile route through tortuous rock gullies of the Shinarump ledge which rises sharply from the river on the left bank. The steep, hard rock surface defied leveling attempts; a road of sorts was dug, picked, and blasted into what still looks like giant rock stairs. Veteran wagon drivers, well-acquainted with frontier roads, called Lee's Backbone the worst road they had ever traveled.

When a wagon finally reached the summit of Lee's Backbone heading

Imaginary picture of Lee's Backbone. *From S. C. Richardson,* In Desert Arizona, *(Independence, Mo., 1938) p. 81*

47

south, the driver had to face a frightening, teeth-jarring descent of 350 feet to the Marble Platform. Frequently the trip from the river over the Backbone and down to the Platform would consume an entire day. If a wagon was damaged enroute, the trip took even longer (see Tour Site No. 13).

Since the worst of Lee's Backbone lay at its lowest part, Warren Johnson traced out an alternate route through softer formations above the Shinarump. Working by hand, it took Johnson and his occasional assistants from 1885 to 1888 to complete the bypass, which joined the old Backbone road about half-way up. Although quite steep in places, the bypass offered the advantage of a smoother surface, and was probably preferred.

Of more value perhaps to passing emigrants was the alternate ferry site, located below the mouth of the Paria. A crossing made here completely bypassed Lee's Backbone by way of a quarter-mile long dugway on the left bank leading from the river up an almost sheer precipice to the Marble Platform. In 1878 the Church sent a quarryman to construct the dugway, which was completed late in the year. From that time until 1898, the lower ferry site was used continually except in times of high water, when the south side landing was submerged (see Tour Site No. 16).

In 1878, the first emigrants bound for Mesa, Arizona, paused along Lee's Backbone to chisel this inscription.

48

After 1878 arriving ferry passengers always hoped that the lower ferry would be in operation. If this crossing site happened to be closed due to high water, it meant they would have to traverse Lee's Backbone, and they frequently complained bitterly to the ferryman.

Ferryboats could be used for only a limited period. Sometimes boats were lost in accidents, but more often they became waterlogged and unwieldy and had to be replaced. In 1881 Church officials decided that a large boat capable of holding two wagons would be ideal. Apparently they did not ask an opinion of Warren Johnson, who would have to propel the boat with 12-foot sweeps. Once across the river, he would then have to drag it upriver to the starting point. Eventually the large boat was built, but Johnson could make little use of such an unwieldy craft. During this period, most of his crossings were made by skiff.

Fortunately for Johnson, the Church sent him assistants, the best of whom was Johnson's own brother-in-law, David Brinkerhoff. Brinkerhoff stayed from 1881 until 1886, when he was appointed bishop at Tuba City. Other assistants came and left at frequent intervals.

After completion of the Mormon temple at St. George in 1877, a new class of travelers began using the Utah-Arizona road. Young Mormon couples from the Arizona settlements began traveling north to have their marriages solemnized in the temple. So many couples did this that the road was referred to as the "Honeymoon Trail." It has been reported that many couples, having visited the temple, were seen heading back home to Arizona, apparently in no hurry whatsoever.[5]

10 OUTLAW GANGS

An important river crossing like Lee's Ferry is eventually visited by a full share of humanity, including those on the wrong side of the law. Just how many known or unknown criminals used the river crossing can never be told. Two stories, however, are worthy of retelling.

In the early 1880s, a trio of outlaws—Tom McCarty, Matt Warner, and Josh Sweat—met in a saloon at Fort Wingate to make plans. All three were from villages in southern Utah. Tom McCarty, in fact, had been involved in the Grass Valley shootings of 1874 that led to the Mormon-Navajo friction and to the building of Lee's Ferry Fort.

Their plan was simple. They would steal a few hundred head of horses in Mexico, drive them north, then sell them to ranchers. Their plan worked once, but when they tried it again, their trail was followed by U.S. deputy marshals who reached the outlaw camp one morning just before dawn. In the shootout that followed, John Sweat was severely wounded in the chest, arm, and leg. The marshals, however, withdrew after the outlaws killed four of the seven lawmen present. A posse was soon organized to follow the outlaw trail, which headed north toward the Colorado River.

In spite of his wounds, Sweat was able to ride in what turned out to be a three hundred-mile horse race to Lee's Ferry. At one point the posse got ahead and prepared an ambush at a spring, but the outlaws detected the trap and slipped on by. At another point a marshal rode close enough to shoot one of the trio's extra horses.

When they reached the crest of Lee's Backbone the outlaws could see the posse only a couple of miles to the rear. They knew by then that they could reach the river in advance of the lawmen, but where would the ferryboat be? If they had to signal for the ferry, then wait for the boat to reach them, they would surely be apprehended.

Galloping their horses the final distance they reached the river to find that the boat was in the middle of the river moving slowly in their direction. One of the outlaws hollered to the ferryman (probably Warren Johnson), "I'll bet you fifty dollars you can't make it the rest of the way in two minutes."

Johnson yelled his acceptance of the bet and put his back to the big sweeps. He won the money, but just as the trio led their horses aboard, Johnson looked up the trail and said, "Let's wait awhile. I see a dust up the road. It might be someone that wants to go over and I can take you all at once." At Johnson's innocent remark the three pulled their guns on the boatman, stating, "Get going. We don't wait for nobody."

By the time the posse reached the riverbank, Johnson and the outlaws were halfway across the river. The marshals yelled for Johnson to return, but with three guns on him he couldn't very well comply. Furthermore, the marshals couldn't shoot for fear of hitting the ferryman.

Once across, McCarty, Warner, and Sweat felt quite secure. With the river too wide to shoot across, and with Johnson as their captive, they relaxed, took a bath, ate a hot meal, and had a good night's sleep—all within sight of the helpless marshals.

Next morning they saddled up and rode north, taking Johnson with them. About five miles from Lee's Ferry they released the unfortunate boatman, but one report says they tied his hands behind him and close-hobbled his feet. It took Johnson two days of rolling and falling to return to Lee's Ferry. With this time lead over the officers, the three outlaws made good their escape into Utah, where they split up—McCarty and Sweat going to Nevada and Warner heading for the Vernal area.

Details of the story were provided by Josh Sweat and Matt Warner years later in separate interviews. Although their versions differed on some minor points, they agreed closely on major details.[1]

Before the decade of the 1880s was out, another group of outlaws tried to escape across Lee's Ferry, only this time they were not so lucky.

On the cold, snow-filled night of March 20, 1889, four masked men took command of the eastbound express of the Atlantic and Pacific Railroad when the train stopped briefly at remote Canyon Diablo in the desert east of Flagstaff. Within a few minutes the four had forced an employee to open a safe, from which the outlaws scooped up all the money in sight plus a substantial amount of jewelry, and had ridden off into the night, apparently heading south.

The four, John J. Smith, Dan Harvick, Bill Stiren, and John Halford, were lately tough cowhands of the famous Hashknife outfit of northern Arizona. Winter boredom had given them an itch for action, which resulted in the train robbery. Smith was apparently the leader.

After dividing the meager bundle of stolen cash they split up, agreeing to meet again in Wyoming. In pairs they rode off, Stiren and Harvick together and Smith and Halford together. From Canyon Diablo they traveled south to throw off pursuers, but they soon turned north toward the Colorado River.[2]

Little did the four know that they were being followed even before the robbery. On their way to Canyon Diablo they had broken into a ranch house, helped themselves to supplies, and made a general mess. When Will C. Barnes, the ranch owner, discovered the break-in, he set out to follow the thieves. Barnes and one of his cowboys, William Broadbent, were able to track the outlaws south, then north, across the Little Colorado River and all the way to Lee's Ferry.[3]

Surprisingly, no one at the ferry had seen any suspicious horsemen, whether in groups of two or four. Not until the capture of the outlaws days later was it learned that Stiren and Harvick had bribed a passing traveler to cross on the ferry, then after dark take the boat back to the south side of the river where it was left waiting. With the hooves of their horses muffled by cloth, Stiren and Harvick quietly crossed the river and headed north. One or both of them must have been familiar with Lee's Ferry, for they headed up the hard-to-find Domínguez Pass over the Echo Cliffs.

With their horses nearly spent, Barnes and Broadbent gave up the chase at Lee's Ferry, but as they rode south they met a posse headed by the energetic young sheriff of Yavapai County, William O. "Buckey" O'Neill. O'Neill had also followed the dim trail, and although he was still two days behind the outlaws, he was closing in fast.

O'Neill predicted that the outlaws would have to visit at least one of the isolated communities in southern Utah—probably either Cannonville or Pahreah. He and his men crossed on the ferry, followed up the Paria to Domínguez Pass, and headed directly for Cannonville. So fast was O'Neill traveling, however, that he unknowingly passed the outlaws and

William O. "Buckey" O'Neill, sheriff of Yavapai County, Arizona, relentlessly pursued train robbers across Lee's Ferry and into Utah in 1889. *Courtesy Arizona Historical Foundation*

reached Cannonville before they did. Puzzled as to how he had missed them, he headed back south trying to pick up the trail.

Soon after O'Neill left, Stiren and Harvick rode into Cannonville, posing as itinerant cowhands. They asked a local inhabitant if they could spend the night, were shown into a house, and were surprisingly confronted with the sight of their two fellow outlaws, Halford and Smith. Although they pretended not to know each other, the Mormon residents were suspicious.

After the four strangers had gone to bed, a group of Mormon men surrounded the house. Capturing three of them was simple, but Smith pulled a hidden gun and took charge. Instantly the Mormons laid down their arms while the four saddled up and rode, laughing, out of town.

A messenger who caught up with O'Neill and his posse told them that the outlaws had been captured in Cannonville, so the sheriff headed back north, arriving soon after the train robbers had escaped. Now Buckey O'Neill was on a hot trail, which led again to the south, astonishingly back toward Lee's Ferry. He passed a camp where the fire was still burning, and realized that his quarry was not far ahead.

On a barren, rocky point over Wahweap Canyon the outlaws had become rimrocked. Just as they were starting to backtrack to find a place to descend, O'Neill and his men came riding up. Confronted by the lawmen, the outlaws opened fire but hit no one. Realizing the desperate situation, Smith attempted to charge through the line on his fast horse, but O'Neill shot the horse dead. At this point Halford and Stiren surrendered. Harvick and Smith, however, jumped over the edge of the rocky point and ran headlong down the steep talus slope. O'Neill and his men fired at them many times, but without effect. O'Neill's posse found a way to descend on their horses, and spent the rest of the day and part of the night following occasional boot tracks in bits of soft ground between the rocks. The next day they began to find tracks of bare feet, then traces of blood. Apparently, long distance hiking in cowboy boots was so painful that the fleeing men chose to go barefoot over the rough rocks.

Smith and Harvick were approaching Domínguez Pass above Lee's Ferry when they found the small water hole known as Willow Tanks. They stopped, soaked their feet, and managed to put their boots on. Just as they were about to continue on down into the Paria Canyon, a rifle cracked and a bullet hit the rocks. Although the outlaws took cover and opened fire, O'Neill was not to be denied. The sheriff rode his big roan right toward Smith, firing as rapidly as possible. Under the onslaught, Smith couldn't even take proper aim. Suddenly the sheriff was almost on top of him, and Smith found himself looking up a rifle barrel at Buckey O'Neill. Naturally, Smith surrendered.

With Smith in custody, O'Neill turned to the other outlaw. "You're next," he yelled to Harvick. A few shots were fired, but with the sheriff and his men advancing, Harvick realized the hopelessness of his situation and threw up his hands.

O'Neill had a difficult time getting his prisoners to Prescott. He took them first to Kanab, then to Milford, where he boarded a train for Salt Lake City. The rest of the way was by train through Denver, south into New Mexico, and finally into Arizona. It was late at night when the train neared the Colorado-New Mexico border. O'Neill and his deputies had dozed off in their chairs. Smith managed to slip a shackle off one leg and to jump off the train as it was climbing a hill. O'Neill and his men were quickly awakened by the cold air from the window, but Smith had escaped in the darkness. Smith made it into Texas, but he "borrowed" a horse that didn't belong to him and was jailed for horse stealing. After a bit of checking, he was found to be the escaped train robber. O'Neill personally went to Texas to bring Smith back.

Thus ended Buckey O'Neill's most celebrated outlaw chase. The epilogue, however, had an ironic twist. Because he had conducted much of the chase in Utah, where he had no jurisdiction, the Yavapai County Board of Supervisors, backed by a court decision, forced the sheriff to pay over two thousand dollars of his own expenses.

Strangest of all—not even O'Neill realized that robbers Smith and Harvick had actually returned to Arizona when they were captured on the mesa above Lee's Ferry. O'Neill's case was better than he knew.

11 ZANE GREY MEETS JIM EMETT

Outlaws could be troublesome, but they were such infrequent visitors that Warren Johnson thought little about them. Ordinary life at Lee's Ferry involved enough hardship and worry to occupy a man's time. Maintaining the roads and keeping a leaky ferryboat in operation were only parts of Johnson's responsibility. The ranch also demanded his time. Labor required on the diversion dam, on the long ditch and flume, and in the fields was endless. Although growing children could and did help out with some of the work, Johnson and his two wives endured much toil and trouble.

In May 1891, a family traveling from Richfield, Utah, to Tuba City paused for a night at the Johnson house. They told Johnson that one of their children had suddenly died on the way and that they had buried the child in Panguitch. Cause of death was then unknown.

About four days later, Johnson's five-year-old boy, Jonathan, was suddenly stricken with sore throat and fever. Then two daughters, Laura Alice and Permelia "Millie," ages seven and nine, fell ill. Jonathan choked to death in his father's arms. Then both of the girls died. Finally, fifteen-year-old Melinda caught the disease and died. A son and three daughters had thus died between May 19 and June 5.

The disease was diphtheria. The passing family, after burying their child in Panguitch, had not known enough to disinfect themselves, their clothing, or their wagon. Three of Johnson's other children caught the diptheria, but eventually recovered.

In 1895, Johnson and the L.D.S. Church authorities reached a mutual conclusion that Johnson's mission at Lee's Ferry had ended. He prepared to move to Kanab to take up a new life. While inspecting a ranch for prospective purchase, a hay rack he was riding upset, throwing him to the ground. Johnson landed on his spine and was paralyzed from the waist down for the rest of his life.

Undeterred by his handicap, Johnson changed his plans and moved his family to Wyoming in 1896 to set up a ranching operation. The difficult life, however, proved too much for him, and during the severe winter of 1902 he died. He was buried at Byron, Wyoming. An unspectacular man, Warren Johnson nonetheless deserves tribute for his steady competence and for the great amount of physical labor he applied to his mission at Lee's Ferry.[1]

Attractive school teacher Sadie Staker (left) watches her pupils at the Lee's Ferry School about 1898. Children are members of the James Emett and Bill Lamb families. *Courtesy Mrs. Cora Brown, Monroe, Utah*

Passengers were always relieved when the ferryboat completed the dangerous river crossing. *Courtesy Southern California Edison Company*

Church authorities replaced Johnson with a rugged veteran of frontier life named James Emett. Born in a covered wagon, he was ever the outdoorsman, uncomfortable in houses, strong, and resilient. Zane Grey, who met Emett in 1907, once wrote a story about the tough ferryman entitled "The Man Who Influenced Me Most," in which he stated, "[Emett] stood well over six feet, and his leonine build, ponderous shoulders, and great shaggy head and white beard gave an impression of tremendous virility and dignity....He had a grave, kindly countenance, rugged and strong."[2] Grey thought that Emett possessed "a strange gift of revelation... connected with his profound psychic and religious powers." Like Warren Johnson, Emett was a practicing polygamist; his two wives bore him eighteen children. Emett had been a rancher and at one time was superintendent of the Canaan Cooperative Stock Company operating on the Arizona Strip.[3]

At the time he was given the Lee's Ferry assignment, Emett was forty-six. While no longer a youth, he was still in his prime both physically and mentally. Arriving in 1896, he quickly concluded that many modifications were needed at Lee's Ferry. With the help of his older children he did everything himself, whether it involved carpentry, blacksmithing, leather tanning, stone masonry, or farming. Among other tasks he built a new ferryboat.

For twenty-three years at Lee's Ferry, the ferryboat was simply a flat bottom barge that was actually rowed across. The oars were made of 2" x 6" boards, bolted together, with a 2" x 10" board on the end that dipped into the water. Frank Johnson, son of Warren, said that it was agony to have to pull on these oars, or sweeps, for very long. Of course the current would push the boat downstream as it crossed, so that the ferryman, after letting off his passengers, would have to tow the boat

56

back upstream with great labor for about a quarter mile before he could start back across.

A track cable was the natural answer. Why it was not put in during the earlier years remains a mystery. When properly rigged with connecting ropes or cables and when angled slightly upstream, the current would actually push the boat across. Also, the boat would not drift downstream.

In 1896 Emett convinced Church authorities that a track cable was necessary. A big two-inch diameter cable consisting of only six strands was brought in, and several men were hired to stretch it across the river. But the cable was simply too big and too heavy for them to handle. Therefore they carefully removed three of the strands—half of the cable —and managed to put it across and to anchor it firmly in rock. As expected, the cable made crossing the river much easier and safer.

Warren Johnson had long thought about building a dugway (a road notched into a steep slope) on the southern approach to the ferry so that travelers would not have to cross either Lee's Backbone or the steep, tortuous bypass Johnson had built. Just before he left, Johnson had laid out the dugway and had even done some work on it, but it was far from finished.

When Emett arrived he shortly concluded that completion of the dugway was a necessity and asked the Church to provide it. Undoubtedly, one of his arguments was that the ferryboat was by then locked onto the track cable at the upper ferry site, making the lower ferry site virtually useless. Emett was apparently persuasive, for a contract to build the road was let in 1898 to a construction firm in Richfield, Utah, for about $1200. The final product wasn't much of a road, being only ten to twelve feet wide, but it served as the main highway for the next thirty years.

Built in soft earth, the dugway was always subject to washout and rock-falls from above as an account by some state officials on an automobile trip in 1915 indicates:

[We] encountered serious difficulty in going down the dugway into Lee's Ferry. Heavy storms had washed the road considerably, requiring much work to make it passable. The most serious setback was a large boulder, weighing a couple of tons, that had been dropped in the middle of the ten foot dugway. It was necessary to blast this in order to get past.[4]

Apparently dynamite had to be included in ordinary automobile supplies!

Unused since 1928, the dugway is still clearly visible as a line beginning at the gauging station and rising slowly until it reaches the Marble Platform about one and a half miles away (see Tour Site No. 15).

Emett was also active in the ranching business, keeping his stock in House Rock Valley. There he competed for the range with the Grand Canyon Cattle Company, led by B. F. Saunders and Charles Dimmick.

Even though the valley was mostly public domain, the company acted aggressively to control water holes and available grazing land. Jim Emett was not a big cattle operator, but he was nonetheless an irritation to the company.

In 1906 the company filed a complaint against Emett charging him with cattle theft. Charles Dimmick was the chief accusing witness. In a noted jury trial in Flagstaff, Emett denied the charge, stating that he was not in House Rock Valley at the time specified, and that, at any rate, the cattle were his own. In April 1907, the jury found Emett not guilty.[5]

It was at the Flagstaff trial that Zane Grey first met Jim Emett. Grey waited out the verdict, then rode with Emett back to Lee's Ferry. Also in the group was Charles Jesse Jones, known generally as "Buffalo" Jones. It was Jones who had encouraged Grey to come out west to participate in a mountain lion hunt on the Kaibab Plateau.

At that time, Buffalo Jones was a famous hunter, adventurer, lecturer, and wildlife expert. Among more routine exploits, he had founded Garden City, Kansas, hunted musk ox during a Yukon winter, and served as game warden at Yellowstone National Park. In House Rock Valley he had established a buffalo ranch to experiment with "cattalo," the hybrid offspring of buffalo and cattle. The cattalo experiment failed, however, because of persistence of the buffalo hump in the fetus, which made for a difficult, if not impossible, birth. By 1907 Jones had concluded his experiments and had sold his buffalo to his partner, James "Uncle Jim" Owens.[6]

From these experiments has evolved today's Buffalo Ranch, located in southern House Rock Valley twenty-eight miles from highway 89a, and run by the Arizona Game and Fish Commission. The present herd is maintained at about two hundred buffalo.

Arriving late at Lee's Ferry, Zane Grey awoke the next morning ready to explore.

> Dawn opened my eyes to what seemed the strangest and most wonderful place in the world. Emett's home was set at the edge of a luxuriant oasis, green with foliage and alfalfa, colored by bright flowers, and shut in on three sides by magnificent red walls three thousand feet high. The thundering Colorado formed a fourth side and separated the oasis from another colossal wall across the river. Paria Creek ran down from the cliffs to water this secluded and desert-bound spot. The low long cabins, crude and picturesque, were shaded by a grove of old cottonwoods, spreading and gnarled, like the oaks of the Druids.[7]

Later that day, Emett, Buffalo Jones, and Grey rode off toward the Kaibab Plateau for the scheduled lion hunt. On their second day out they reached a spring in House Rock Valley (apparently Jacob Pools), where the Grand Canyon Cattle Company had built a small rock cabin. As they were dismounting in front of the cabin, Grey heard Emett utter a "deep, fierce imprecation." Grey turned and saw Emett holding his six-gun on a man who had just emerged from the cabin. It was Charlie Dimmick, who had accused Emett of cattle rustling. In Dimmick's hands was a rifle.

Grey wrote that he acted instinctively, stepping out between the two men. "Don't kill each other," he said, "it'll spoil my trip."

Emett immediately sheathed his gun and walked away. Dimmick could only say to Grey, "Howdy, young feller! You shore took chances heah!." Later Buffalo Jones told Grey that Emett and Dimmick would someday kill each other if they ever met again. Fortunately, they never did.[8]

Emett predicted that the untamed desert country around Lee's Ferry would capture Zane Grey's imagination, that the land would form a backdrop for many stories Grey would write. The "revelation" was, to say the least, highly accurate. In many of his books, Grey seems to be describing House Rock Valley, the Kaibab, or the red-rock canyons to the east. In his first book about the West, *The Last of the Plainsmen,* which was nonfiction, Grey wrote a biography of Buffalo Jones. In a later fiction work, *Heritage of the Desert,* he centered the story about a place easily recognized as Lee's Ferry—with a white-bearded patriarch thrown in!

What the Grand Canyon Cattle Company could not accomplish with court action they did with money. In August 1909, the company bought the ferry from the Church of Jesus Christ of Latter-day Saints, thus putting Emett out of business. Emett acceded the next month by selling his ranch and other holdings at Lee's Ferry to the company.[9]

Lee's Ferry had been a key link between Mormon settlements in Utah and Arizona, but by 1900 most people who had to travel a long distance between these states went by railroad. The train trip through either Colorado or California, though much longer in miles, was much shorter in time. By 1909 traffic along the historic wagon road and across the ferry was almost entirely local in character. The once-vital link that had served Church interests for so long was no longer needed.

12 THE ENGINEER— ROBERT B. STANTON

Let us now backtrack a few years to midsummer 1889, the first of July. Warren Johnson was still operating Lee's Ferry. On that day sixteen men in three boats seemed to come out of nowhere, descending the river from Glen Canyon. At Lee's Ferry they tied up, got out, and made plans for their next move. One of the group, Frank Mason Brown, apparently rented a team and wagon from Johnson and drove away toward Kanab for supplies.

During the week-long wait for Brown to return, the other men told Johnson the incredible story of this expedition. In a nutshell, this group was the working nucleus of the newly-formed Denver, Colorado Canyon, and Pacific Railroad Company. Their mission on the river was to survey for a possible railroad route *right through the canyons* from Grand Junction, Colorado, to the lower Colorado River, then across southern California to San Diego.[1]

The chief engineer was Robert Brewster Stanton, a civil engineer who had specialized in building difficult mountain railroads and who was convinced that the "water level" route would prove feasible. Although Stanton directed all field operations, the man actually in charge was Frank M. Brown, the company president.

On their voyage down the river toward Lee's Ferry, the Brown-Stanton party had suffered many accidents, most of them in the wild rapids of Cataract Canyon. Two of their five boats had been sunk, and they had lost most of their supplies.

In his journal, Stanton complained about the "light, brittle, cedar hunting and pleasure boats" that Brown had supplied them with. What Stanton didn't mention was that the round-bottom boats were simply unstable in white water. Yet with only three of these inadequate boats left, the party was preparing for an even more hazardous voyage through Marble and Grand Canyons. To make matters worse, they carried no life preservers!

Brown finally returned with supplies, and on July 9, 1889, the group left Lee's Ferry to continue the survey. They didn't get far before tragedy struck. Somehow the boats made it through Badger Creek and Soap Creek Rapids, but just below the latter rapid, Frank Brown and crewman Harry McDonald were caught by an eddy current in midstream. Without warning the cross current flipped the boat over, spilling the men into the water. Without a life preserver, Brown sank quickly to his death. McDonald, who managed to reach the left bank, ran for help. Stanton, close behind in another skiff, could do nothing more than retrieve Brown's notebook, which bobbed to the surface. This quick and fateful accident happened just twelve miles downstream from Lee's Ferry.

Perhaps not realizing that his round-bottom boats were dangerously inappropriate, chief engineer Stanton made a major error by deciding to continue on into Marble Canyon.

On July 15, two crewmen, Peter M. Hansbrough and Henry Richards were caught in a current that welled up against a rock wall at Mile 25.2.

In their efforts to push away from the wall, the two men capsized the boat, and both were quickly drowned.

After this second tragic accident, Stanton decided to abandon the voyage. Near Vasey's Paradise, thirty-two miles below Lee's Ferry, the boats and supplies were cached. Then Stanton and his men climbed out to the west by way of a narrow side canyon. Reaching the floor of House Rock Valley, they walked north to the VT Ranch at the base of the Kaibab Plateau. From there they traveled to Kanab and finally reached Denver.

By this time Stanton himself was completely sold on the idea of building a watergrade railroad down the canyons. His enthusiasm convinced the New York financiers, who agreed to back him on a second voyage. Stanton even bought an interest in the company. Exceptionally heavy boats were constructed with watertight compartments. Furthermore, life preservers were included among the supplies.

Stanton's second expedition put into the river at the mouth of North Wash, near the head of Glen Canyon, on December 10, 1889, with the group expected to spend the winter months on the Colorado completing the survey.

Traveling in three boats, Stanton and his eleven men arrived at Lee's Ferry on a windy afternoon, December 23. There they made camp near the old fort, rested, and began preparations for the next part of the trip.

Robert B. Stanton (left, at end of table) and his men eat Christmas dinner, 1889, beside Lee's Ferry Fort, before resuming their railroad survey through the canyons of the Colorado River. *Courtesy Utah State Historical Society*

For Christmas dinner they set up a table in front of the fort and had a regal feast: turkey, beef, ox heart, chicken, Colorado River salmon, plum pudding, cake and pie—much of it courtesy of Warren Johnson and his wives.

Three days later they shoved off and by December 31 had passed the point where Frank Brown was drowned. But they were to have troubles of their own. The next day, January 1, 1890, photographer Franklin A. Nims, while trying to climb high enough to include all three boats in his shot, fell from a ledge, breaking his leg and cracking his skull. Obviously Nims had to be taken out of the canyon.

Through a side canyon, Stanton ascended to House Rock Valley and proceeded to Lee's Ferry, where he arrived about midnight. The next morning, Warren Johnson hitched up his team and wagon for the rough trip to the canyon rim. Meanwhile Stanton's men were taking Nims up the steep, rough west side of House Rock Canyon. Occasionally the stretcher had to be swung along by ropes around and over vertical drops.

Finally, with Nims taken care of and with Stanton himself now acting as photographer, the expedition resumed its voyage. Although there were many more adventures (including a smashed boat), no lives were lost. Stanton felt his trip had been a complete success. The initial survey for the D.C.C. & P. Railroad had been completed, and, for the doughty engineer, the results were highly favorable. Possibly Stanton could almost hear the steam engines rumbling through the canyons, carrying coal from Colorado to the industrial plants of the Pacific Coast.

New York financiers might have been intrigued by Stanton's dream, but when it came time to put up millions of dollars for railroad construction, they backed out. Stanton campaigned for a few years, but finally turned his attention to other enterprises.[2]

While in Glen Canyon, he had noticed fine particles of gold in the sand of the river bed. Attracted by the placer gold possibilities, he then began construction of a massive dredge to extract these gold particles. While the dredge was under construction near present-day Bullfrog Marina, Stanton boated up and down Glen Canyon, staking out claims he expected to mine with a whole fleet of such dredges.[3]

Some of Stanton's claims were located just upstream from Lee's Ferry, one of the few places that he could reach by land. In 1899 Stanton had his men put in a road along the left (south) river bank from the ferry upstream about one and one-half miles. The road, which goes nowhere and serves no purpose, is still visible today. Stanton's only reason for building it was to "prove up" his claims in the area by doing required assessment work (see Tour Site No. 11).

Unfortunately for Stanton, his big dredge operation was a failure. Gold was certainly present, but in such fine particles that it would not settle on the amalgamators. In late 1901 Stanton ceased all operations, abandoned his dredge, and placed his company in receivership.

Although Robert B. Stanton's mining operations were the most extensive at the time, much prospecting and mining occurred in Glen Canyon and in the San Juan River Canyon in the 1880s and 1890s. During these years many prospectors passed Lee's Ferry, either on their way in or out of the canyon. Most of their efforts were concentrated on gravel bars lying several feet above the river. Some gold was found, but few, if any, struck it rich. Most prospectors soon discovered that expenses almost always exceeded income. By 1900 only an occasional prospector was seen along the river above Lee's Ferry.[4]

A few men, like Stanton, believed that the gold in the sands of the Colorado could be recovered with better technology and equipment. Stanton found that even with his big investments, the technology of 1900 was not equal to the task. A few years later, however, another man even more visionary perhaps than Stanton, felt he had the answer. His name was Charles H. Spencer.

13 THE PROMOTER— CHARLES H. SPENCER

Charles H. Spencer is an enigma in the history of the canyons. Although he pursued the quest for gold, he seemed to enjoy the pursuit more than the gold, especially when he was spending other people's money. A product of the wilderness, Spencer obviously had a thirst for adventure, a love for wild scenery, and a passion for freedom. Virtually unschooled himself, Spencer's attitude toward so-called "experts" bordered on disgust, since they seemed to lack imagination.

Charlie Spencer could and did endure harsh weather, lack of food, and hostile Indians. He performed heavy, back-breaking toil, and, above all, he did almost everything as well if not better than any of his men. Following him into the wilderness with only a vague promise of future pay, they eagerly pursued his schemes, and, when all had failed, they spoke well of him.[1]

In 1909 Spencer and his men set up a crusher and amalgamator on the San Juan River, about 125 river miles above Lee's Ferry. Their object was to extract gold from rocks of the Wingate formation, a deep red, broken sandstone frequently exposed in the canyon country. After some

Charles H. Spencer promoted great sums of money to bring mechanized mining to Lee's Ferry. *Courtesy Charles H. Spencer*

laborious testing, however, someone discovered that the Chinle formation, lying just below the Wingate, contained as much, if not more, gold. Moreover, the purple and gray banded Chinle was easily loosened with water and could be sluiced with high pressure hoses. Their only question then was where to find sufficient fuel to run the machinery.

At this point two wandering prospectors appeared, discussed the problem with Spencer, and suggested moving the operations to Lee's Ferry. The Chinle shale, they pointed out, was also exposed at Lee's Ferry. Furthermore, coal deposits were known to exist in the cliffs a few miles to the northeast. Quickly realizing that the coal could fuel boilers to pump water to sluice the Chinle, Charlie headed for Lee's Ferry.

Spencer and some of his men were led by a Navajo over an old Indian trail across rugged country near Navajo Mountain to the eastern base of the Echo Cliffs. Then their trail led them across a succession of deep, dry gullies just south of the Echo Peaks, finally cresting the ridge just east of the peaks. At this point the Navajo guide picked up a stone and tossed it on a large pile of stones. He said that every passing Navajo added a stone in commemoration of a battle between the Utes and Navajos in this vicinity years ago.

Someone remarked that this old Indian trail was the "Buzzard's Highline." The name caught on and was applied to the trail which was so known for many years.[2] Today this trail is all but forgotten. Except at certain points, it is so faint that it is almost impossible to follow (see Tour Site No. 18).

From the crest of the Echo Cliffs, Spencer and his men obtained their first view of Lee's Ferry, about two thousand feet below. From that point the Buzzard's Highline trail led down the immense sand slope to the Colorado, which the men followed a mile and a half downstream to the ferry. Arriving in May 1910, Spencer immediately studied prospects of the Chinle shale, here exposed as a wide strata about three hundred yards from the river behind the old fort. The river would provide water. A boiler and pumps could be installed to convey water under high pressure to sluice the shale. Charlie's only question at this point was fuel; where were the reputed seams of coal?

After examining several dry but rugged canyons, Spencer's men finally located a sizeable vein of coal on a distant branch of Warm Creek, a tributary of the Colorado twenty-eight miles upstream in Glen Canyon. Eager to test the gold prospects, Spencer began his experiments at Lee's Ferry even before he obtained coal, using driftwood for fuel.[3]

First he experimented with a "pipe dredge," a device that injected air and water under high pressure directly down into the ground, forcing sand and fine particles up through a casing. Spencer tried the pipe dredge on a gravel bed near the river bank, but he had great difficulty making it work. Just below the surface the dredge hit coarse rock and

65

Charlie Spencer's pack outfit crosses the river at Lee's Ferry in May, 1910. Note the lifeboat in tow. *Courtesy A. H. Jones, Elizabeth, Colorado*

would sink no further. The experiment was given up as a failure.

Undaunted, Spencer went ahead with his plan to recover gold from the Chinle by sluicing the shale over an amalgamator. A big boiler and pumps near the river's edge were activated, and water was pumped through hoses to high pressure nozzles aimed at the shale. The water dissolved the soft Chinle and carried it down a long flume back toward the river where an amalgamator was set up.

It should be mentioned here that the Chinle shale does in fact contain small amounts of gold in the form of "dust," or very small particles. In terms of value the gold runs only a few cents for each cubic yard of shale. Spencer, of course, was working on the assumption that the values would prove to be much higher.

Spencer's first "runs" of shale over the amalgamators were made in the spring of 1911. At first everything worked fine, but it soon became

Charlie Spencer's "industrial area" at Lee's Ferry was built to process gold from the Chinle shale. At far right is the Lee's Ferry Fort. The photo was taken in 1914. *Courtesy Dock Marston, San Francisco*

Water pumped from the Colorado River is directed against the Chinle shale at Lee's Ferry by employees of Charles H. Spencer. The photo was taken in 1911. *Courtesy Charles H. Spencer*

apparent that the mercury in the amalgamator was becoming clogged. Instead of being absorbed by the mercury, the gold was passing on out with the tailings. The plates were scraped, new mercury was applied, and more material was sluiced across them. The same result. What in the complex Chinle formation was causing a film to form on the mercury? Tests were suspended until a chemical analysis could be run.

Numerous efforts were made to solve the problem, but nothing was successful. Several of Spencer's chemists made tests, and samples were sent to outside experts. Spencer said later that he even sent samples to the famous Madame Curie in Paris, who reported the presence of a foreign element that could not be identified.[4]

Even with this setback Spencer would not admit the possibility of failure. While chemists and mining engineers wrestled with the problem, he shifted his crew to bringing coal to Lee's Ferry.

At first Spencer thought that mules might be used to haul coal from the mines on Warm Creek. With this in mind he ordered his men to build the incredible trail up the steep Echo Cliffs immediately east of his mining operations at Lee's Ferry. Spencer and his men knew about and frequently used Domínguez Pass, but it was difficult. In addition, the trail to the pass started two and one-half miles up the Paria. Certainly a good trail right above the work site would be an improvement.

The trail was actually built during the late summer and fall of 1910, by men using shovels, picks, and crowbars.[5] On at least one occasion, Spencer used the trail construction to promote his enterprise financially. He told the men that a group of investors from Chicago were coming for a visit and asked them to put on a good and noisy show. When these officials were observed to arrive at the river bank, the workmen on the trail began setting off sticks of dynamite, one every few minutes. When the investors left they were apparently quite satisfied that Spencer's workmen were earning their money.[6]

Spencer later claimed that the trail was laid out by his white mule, Pete. "I just told him what to do and he started up the cliff. I followed him, marking the trail."[7] While admitting that Pete was a superior mule, none of the workmen could recall later that Pete had anything to do with the trail.

In spite of booming displays for visiting dignitaries, the trail was eventually finished to the top. Spencer and his men used it in preference to the Domínguez Pass trail, but the Spencer trail was never used to carry coal. Nevertheless, it is one of the more spectacular reminders of Charles H. Spencer's mining operations at Lee's Ferry. Although eroded in places, it may still be traversed to the top of the Echo Cliffs (see Tour Site No. 2).

Despite the new trail up the cliffs, Spencer was reluctant to decide on mules to transport coal. If his mining operation were ever to get beyond the experimental state, he would need far more coal than could be provided by such a slow, inefficient system. But there was another way—transportation by water.

The coal vein that had been located on a high branch of Warm Creek canyon lay about twenty miles from the Colorado River. Normally Warm Creek was dry, carrying water only for brief periods after storms. A wagon road, Spencer surmised, could be built down Warm Creek canyon to the river. From there the coal could be moved by boat twenty-eight river miles to Lee's Ferry.

While some men opened the mines, others began building a crude

A six-yoke team of oxen tows a heavy wagon loaded with mining supplies on the dugway leading to Lee's Ferry. "Bull-whackers" beside the oxen urged them on by cracking their whips like firecrackers above the animals' heads. *Courtesy Arizona Department of Archives and Library*

road down Warm Creek. Still others began construction of a barge at its mouth. Sometime during the early fall days of 1911 the first load of coal was taken by ox-drawn wagon down the dry canyon to the Colorado and loaded on the barge. Three or four men took the coal-laden barge from Warm Creek through Glen Canyon to Lee's Ferry, using green aspen poles to push it away from the cliffs.[8]

The obvious question was how to get the barge back upstream for another trip. Logically, a tug boat was needed. A twenty-six-foot launch, christened the *Violet Louise,* was purchased and brought to Lee's Ferry to do the job. Unfortunately, the *Violet Louise* was far too underpowered to push a big barge up a river current or to negotiate the difficult sandbars that lay hidden in the murky water.

At this point one of the Chicago officials from Spencer's company, Dr. Julius Koebig, came up with a novel suggestion: Why not build a big steamboat to carry the coal? Charlie Spencer said later he wasn't consulted on the steamboat idea and didn't even know about it until the boat had been ordered from a firm in San Francisco.

At any rate, the craft agreed upon was to be the largest boat ever afloat on the Colorado River north of the Grand Canyon. In length it was to measure ninety-two feet and in width twenty-five feet. It would have a large steam boiler that would power a twelve-foot wide stern paddlewheel.

Built during 1911 in San Francisco, the steamboat was dismantled, placed on railroad cars, and shipped to the railhead at Marysvale, Utah, fully two hundred miles from the mouth of Warm Creek. When it arrived in Marysvale in September, 1911, the parts were placed on a series of wagons for the rest of the trip.

At a point near Circleville, Utah, lay a tight elbow turn above a steep slope. All the wagons made this difficult turn except the last one carrying the heaviest load, the boiler. The wheels on this last wagon slipped off the road, the chains snapped, and the boiler rolled seventy-five feet down the embankment. It took an entire month and some ingenious methods to drag the boiler up and reposition it on the wagon.[9]

When all parts had finally arrived at the mouth of Warm Creek, the long process of reconstructing the boat was begun under the direction of a shipwright sent from the San Francisco firm. Work was suspended during mid-winter but was finished early in the spring of 1912. Despite Spencer's professed lack of enthusiasm for the boat, the craft was christened the *Charles H. Spencer,* and the name was painted on the bow.

Finding a willing crew for the steamboat was not easy, for few of Spencer's workmen had ever done any boating of this type. Most had backgrounds in farming, ranching, mining, or carpentry, and few of them wished to tempt fate on a steamboat plying the treacherous Colorado

The *Charles H. Spencer* awaits cast-off time at the river bank at Lee's Ferry. On board (left to right) are Pete Hanna, captain; an unidentified crewman, "Rip Van Winkle" Schneider, "Smithy" Smith, Jerry Johnson, Bert Leach, and Al Byers. The photo was taken in 1912. *Courtesy Kolb Bros. Studio, Grand Canyon*

River. Only one, Pete Hanna, who was designated captain, had ever operated a steamboat. Finally a group of reluctant individuals was persuaded to board the steamer for a run downriver to Lee's Ferry.

A few wagons of coal were taken down Warm Creek to the Colorado where the coal was loaded on the main deck of the steamboat. Hanna ordered the boiler fired, and when steam pressure was up, he sounded the whistle. The big stern paddlewheel began to turn. Now it was just twenty-eight miles to go!

About a hundred yards away from the launch point, however, the boat ran hard aground on a hidden sandbar. Working with shovels, the men dug all day to free the unwieldy craft. Night was spent in a rocky cove beneath the cliffs of Glen Canyon.[10]

When they started off the next day, Hanna tried a different technique. He directed that the boat be turned around so as to head upstream, even though it would be moving downstream. In other words, it went *backward* down the river, with the paddlewheel serving to slow its downstream plunge. This method imparted maneuverability and helped avoid further mishaps.

Late that day the *Charles H. Spencer* backed its way into Lee's Ferry, where the workmen on shore cheered its arrival. It thus appeared that the boat had proven itself. However, Pete Hanna, being the cautious type, directed that only a small amount of coal be unloaded, for no one knew how much coal it would take to get back to Warm Creek.

On the return trip it became apparent that the steamboat had to run full steam to make even slow progress against the current. When Warm Creek was reached a check showed that most of the coal had been consumed. It was clear that it took just about all the coal the boat could carry to make the twenty-eight mile upriver run![11]

Hanna and his crew loaded on a few tons of coal, brought the craft back to Lee's Ferry, and tied it up at the bank. Except for Hanna, the crew quit or were assigned to other jobs.

About two months later, Spencer decided to try a different method. He obtained another crew for Hanna, and ordered that the steamboat tow the coal barge up to Warm Creek. In that way, the real payload of coal could be carried on the barge. When this technique was tried it seemed to work as planned. Both the steamer and the barge reached Warm Creek without a problem. Coal was loaded, then three or four men free-floated the barge down to Lee's Ferry. The steamboat followed.[12]

Now that a successful method of using the steamboat had been devised, the *Charles H. Spencer* was tied up until more coal was needed. But more coal was not required. Spencer was never able to extract gold from the Chinle. When the chemists failed to discover why the mercury in the amalgamators quickly clogged and stopped absorbing gold, Spencer's entire operation was doomed. The big steamboat was never used again.

About three years later, in 1915, flood water forced driftwood under the boat. Then when the high water subsided, the boat settled on the driftwood, tipped on its side, and sank in a few feet of water.[13] In later years someone ripped off the superstructure. Today the weathered hull and boiler of the *Charles H. Spencer* lie where they sank, highly visible in today's clear water (see Tour Site No. 3).

Directly north of the old fort about two hundred yards is the scar in the gray Chinle shale made by Spencer's hydraulic sluicing operation. An old boiler used by Spencer lies on the flat near the point where it was used. A number of rock buildings that Spencer erected have since been removed.

While at Lee's Ferry, Charlie Spencer engaged in a number of related enterprises and side operations. For instance, another complete hydraulic

71

and sluicing operation was carried out at the town of Pahreah. It was also used to work on the Chinle shale and encountered the same difficulty.

Rarely was there enough money available to pay the workmen for their work. In lieu of wages Spencer promised his men a certain amount of acreage in an irrigation project he was planning on the Paria River about thirty miles to the north. In his pitch to his men, Spencer would expound on the obvious fertility of the Lee's Ferry Ranch, which obtained its water from the Paria. Thus many men continued on at their mining tasks without pay, dreaming of the day they would become rich landowners.[14]

Charlie Spencer also brought the first automobile into Lee's Ferry. It was a long convertible called a Thomas Royal Flyer, vintage about 1910. For its day it was a very prestigious automobile. Since none of Spencer's men could drive, the company sent along an optional extra— a chauffeur.

To everyone's surprise the Royal Flyer came in from Flagstaff without trouble and was crossed on the ferry. The next day Spencer ordered the chauffeur to return to Flagstaff to pick up some needed chemicals. When days passed and the auto still did not return, Spencer sent out a search party which found the car in a ravine near Flagstaff. The chauffeur had apparently abandoned the car after accidentally veering off the road and breaking an axle. A ten-yoke team of oxen was sent from Lee's Ferry to tow the auto into Flagstaff where it was sold.[15]

Charlie Spencer even had a hand in operating the ferry. After Emett's departure in 1909, the ferryboat was operated by whatever cowhands of the Grand Canyon Cattle Company happened to be at the crossing. That this arrangement provided the public less than optimum service was obvious. Needing reliable ferrymen, the company called on the men most qualified—sons of Warren Johnson.

In February 1910, Jerry Johnson arrived from Wyoming and assumed the role of ferryman. In July Frank Johnson also moved to Lee's Ferry to assist his brother. From that time until the end of ferry service, Johnson family members held official responsibility for its operation.[16]

In June 1910, Coconino County bought the ferry from the cattle company because the county was concerned that the ferry remain a vital link in the highway system, yet the cattle company was reluctant to spend required funds for maintenance.[17]

Even though the Johnson brothers were the official ferrymen, this did not mean that a Johnson always operated the boat. A number of cowhands from the cattle company as well as Spencer's workmen often operated the boat. Charlie Spencer and his men even built a new ferryboat and when necessary made needed repairs to the ferry equipment.

Inexperienced hands, however, sometimes got into trouble. In March 1911, Spencer's men finished installation of a new track cable, and since one of the men had to make a trip to Flagstaff, they decided to take him across the river. No one bothered to summon one of the Johnson brothers from the ranch. Unfamiliar with the ropes and pulleys, the crew allowed the bow rope to become too slack, causing the boat to stop in mid-river and begin to nose under the water. Finally the boat lunged clear under, throwing a team, a wagon, and men overboard. One man, Pres Apperson, was drowned, while the other men reached shore only with great difficulty.[18]

By 1913, almost everyone associated with Spencer had left Lee's Ferry. Spencer himself took on new enterprises in other parts of the country, yet he never forgot the Chinle shale. He eventually learned that what caused the amalgamators to clog up was rhenium, a rare metallic element completely unknown in 1912. Rhenium can be removed by simple procedures discovered long after Spencer left Lee's Ferry. Learning of these techniques in later years, Spencer returned to his still-valid claims at the ghost town of Paria (formerly Pahreah), in the 1960s, when he was over ninety years old. His objective was no longer gold, but the rhenium itself, which is a highly valuable super-conductor of electricity. He and his daughter, Mrs. Muriel Pope, set up camp at Paria and ran a series of chemical tests on the Chinle shale. However, Spencer claimed his success was being blocked by international mining cartels that didn't want his vast body of ore to be put on the market.[19] Whatever the true story, Spencer never struck it rich. Although he is now dead, he will not soon be forgotten. The canyon country has never seen anything quite like him.

Sporadic mining activity has occurred near Lee's Ferry at intervals throughout this century. During the depression of the 1930s, a few prospectors searched for gold in Glen Canyon, but their efforts soon proved fruitless.[20]

During the 1950s hopeful uranium seekers armed with geiger counters swarmed all through the canyon country, looking especially in Shinarump conglomerate, where uranium was often located in petrified wood. At Lee's Ferry, the Shinarump is prominent in Lee's Backbone and in the four hundred-foot high bench below the Vermilion Cliffs. A number of uranium claims were staked, mines were opened, and access roads were bulldozed, but in general, uranium mineralization in the Lee's Ferry area was found to be quite low. The only mine near Lee's Ferry ever to ship ore was the El Pequito, located northwest of the Lee's Ferry Ranch. Within a few years after uranium activity first began, all mines were abandoned and prospecting had entirely ceased.[21]

14 THE DAM BUILDERS

Charlie Spencer once said that Glen Canyon Dam was bound to fail, primarily because it rests on layers of rock strata that contain the Chinle shale, the crumbly, slimy-when-wet formation that Charlie once worked for its gold content. In his nineties when he made the statement, Charlie was not dissuaded by the fact that the Chinle is sandwiched between solid rock layers several hundred feet below the concrete of the dam and that sheer pressure holds all strata in its place. "I don't care what the geologists say; the dam will fail when the water seeps down to the Chinle," Spencer declared.

If the dam had been built where early government engineers first recommended, Charlie might have been right, for the Chinle *is* exposed at Lee's Ferry, and their choice damsite during the 1920s was not far away. In fact the proposed dam was often referred to as the Lee's Ferry Dam.

Before 1914 the great plateau canyons of the river were largely unknown and unvisited by dam builders, who surmised that dams in the big canyons would be prohibitively expensive if not technically impossible.

Anyone with imagination, however, could see the great economic potential of the water then flowing to the sea. As far back as 1890, Major John Wesley Powell, writing of the lower Colorado, predicted:

> If the waters [of the Colorado River] are to be used, great works must be constructed costing millions of dollars, and then ultimately a region of country can be irrigated larger than was ever cultivated along the Nile, and all the products of Egypt will flourish therein.[1]

The art of designing and building dams advanced rapidly during the early 1900s until, by the time of World War I, engineers had gained enough confidence to consider placing a major dam in one of the Colorado River canyons. In an influential report written by hydrologist Eugene "E. C." LaRue of the U.S. Geological Survey in 1916, a number of potential storage reservoirs in the canyons and irrigation projects along tributary streams were suggested.[2]

Irrigation possibilities were important, but so also was the need for main stream flood control, since the erratic Colorado had repeatedly devastated parts of California and Arizona. The high potential for hydroelectric power generation greatly interested urban officials in the larger cities—particularly those in Los Angeles. Thus when engineers set off down the canyons to appraise damsites, they did so with a large measure of public support.

Necessary to any detailed investigation of the canyons were high quality topographic maps that showed exact distances up and down river. This mapping job fell to the Geologic Survey which sent survey crews into each of the major Colorado River canyons. These technicians, together with hydrologists and geologists, were ordered to delineate canyon topography, to examine potential damsites, and to obtain an accurate listing of mileages through each canyon.

Lee's Ferry was chosen as the key point in the mapping survey. Due to its accessibility, as well as its strategic location, it was given Mile Zero designation, with all mileages both up and down stream shown as distances from Lee's Ferry.[3] (Actually, two separate Mile Zeros were used, one-half mile apart. See Tour Site No. 1.)

The products of these surveys, the U.S.G.S. "profile" maps of the canyons, are rarely seen today, but modern adaptations have been made for river runners, such as the excellent river guides published by Westwater Books. These modern versions still use the same mileage designations, with Lee's Ferry shown as Mile Zero.

Since large dams on the Colorado were at last believed feasible, politicians in the seven Colorado Basin states began the long "War for the Colorado," the usually polite but sometimes bitter struggle to obtain water developments for their respective areas.

In this "war," California held the best hand, for its rapid industrial

Enroute from Flagstaff to Lee's Ferry in 1923 to map the Grand Canyon, the government survey crew has to stop and repair the road. *Courtesy U.S. Geological Survey*

75

growth necessarily implied an increasing need for both water and electric power. California's large population and high tax base provided that state with greater political power as compared to the other states in the basin. Of even greater concern, however, was the doctrine of "first in time, first in right," which meant that if California actually diverted and used *all* the water in the river, it would have the right to use all of it thereafter.

To forestall California, representatives of the other states proposed a compact that would apportion the waters equitably. As the first big step toward that objective, the Colorado River Compact was signed in late 1922 in Santa Fe. The Compact has been the virtual law of the river ever since.

In the Compact, Lee's Ferry again played a significant part. Since the states could not agree on a formula to apportion the water state-by-state, they divided the water in what they believed were nearly equal amounts between an arbitrary "Upper Basin" and a corresponding "Lower Basin." The dividing point between the basins was designated as Lee's Ferry. Actually the "Compact Point" was set one mile below the mouth of the Paria River or about two miles below the ferry crossing. In official water matters, the Compact Point is called "Lee Ferry."

In the Compact the Upper Basin agreed to release a specified minimum amount of water over a specified period of time past Lee's Ferry.

Human muscle assists an underpowered truck move the scow *Navajo* through some soft terrain near Lee's Ferry. This scow was used from 1921 to 1923 in the investigation of a damsite in lower Glen Canyon. *Courtesy Southern California Edison Co.*

To accomplish this required an accurate measurement of the water passing that point. Even before the Compact was signed, a water gauging station was established at Lee's Ferry. Anticipating that it might succeed in building a hydroelectric generating dam and powerplant in Glen Canyon to serve the Los Angeles area, the Southern California Edison Company sent crews to Lee's Ferry to set up a gauging station and to begin surveying damsites in July 1921. The U.S. Geological Survey participated and was actually in charge of the station.

Necessary installations for the gauging station included a cable hung on towers across the river, a recorder well and shelter, and living quarters for a resident operator. The largest of Charlie Spencer's old rock cabins was remodeled into a residence, while another was converted into a warehouse. Water measurements were first made in August 1921 and have been recorded daily ever since.[4]

When the gauging station was established, the official in charge was U.S.G.S. hydrologist E. C. LaRue. After writing the 1916 survey report on the river, he had participated in the 1921 mapping survey expedition of Cataract and Glen Canyons, and was busily examining potential damsites. LaRue concluded that the best damsite on the entire Colorado River was at a point just four miles above Lee's Ferry. Just before it reaches the ferry, while still deeply intrenched in Glen Canyon, the river makes a five-mile loop through the sandstone, where air distance is only about a mile.

A dam at Mile 4, LaRue stated, could take advantage of a natural spillway location through the neck of the loop. Water from the reservoir could also be conveyed through the rock neck by penstock to operate a hydroelectric generating plant at Lee's Ferry.[5]

Impressed by LaRue's findings, the Southern California Edison Company worked at Lee's Ferry and at the Mile 4 damsite from 1921 to 1923, collecting data needed for design specifications. A drill crew, using a barge, obtained a number of core samples from the river bed and from the abutments.

In 1925 the U.S.G.S. published an impressive report by LaRue in which he detailed his findings at damsites all along the river. He reported on a damsite in Black Canyon (present site of Hoover Dam), for instance, but concluded that Glen Canyon's Mile 4 was superior.[6]

As the decade of the 1920s wore on, however, arguments prevailed for the building of a dam closer to the southern California electric power market. For one thing, transmission lines would be shorter. In 1928 the Boulder Canyon Project Act, which authorized construction of Hoover Dam, was passed, ending the argument.

Crews from the Southern California Edison Company filed away their drill logs from Glen Canyon and turned their attention elsewhere. At the Lee's Ferry gauging station a succession of operators spent their time beneath the cliffs, measuring the daily flow of the muddy river.

It was evident to most water experts, however, that if the Upper Basin was to have its share of water development projects, a huge storage reservoir had to be built somewhere to even out the erratic river flows. Since the 1922 Compact was quite specific that deliveries of water would be measured at Lee's Ferry, the big reservoir had to be above that point.

It was also apparent that only one potential reservoir site was large enough. A reservoir in Glen Canyon could hold sufficient water from wet years to meet annual Compact requirements for water releases to the Lower Basin, even during a sustained drouth. Water projects further upstream would not have to be shut down in dry years to make the deliveries past Lee's Ferry.[7]

In September 1946, the Bureau of Reclamation sent a field team to Lee's Ferry to make a reconnaissance of potential damsites. Starting at the old Mile 4 damsite located by LaRue in the 1920s, this new crew, led by engineer Vaud Larson, quickly found some basic flaws. The cliffs on either side were badly fractured—poor places to anchor a dam. Also drilling disclosed that the slippery Chinle shale was close to bedrock— obviously a dangerous foundation for a massive dam. In 1947 and 1948 Larson and his men investigated farther upstream and found a much better damsite at Mile 15.3, where Glen Canyon Dam is now located.

Soon after Glen Canyon Dam was authorized in 1956, roads were cut across the mesas to the damsite and to the new town of Page. Lee's Ferry was little touched by the building of the dam which was completed in 1964.

15 LAST DAYS OF THE FERRY

By 1918 automobiles were a fairly common sight at Lee's Ferry, but wagon travel still predominated. Roads south to Flagstaff and northwest to Kanab were extremely bad, even by the standards of the day; surfacing, either with pavement or with gravel, was practically nonexistent. Even main roads were only tracks through the desert.

Under these conditions, a trip through Lee's Ferry was not something to be undertaken lightly. Since few autos then had luggage compartments, drivers wise to desert travel quite liberally festooned their cars

Two men prepare to test their Model T Ford across the mud bank after crossing the river on the ferry. Photo taken about 1922. *Courtesy Dock Marston, San Francisco*

with water bags, tools, spare parts, and emergency survival gear. In reporting an official trip by Coconino County employees in 1919, one participant wrote:

Stuck in sand at Bitter Springs....Reached ferry next noon. River low. Waded and pushed car halfway across to get on ferry boat, and but for a horse hitched on front of car, that vehicle and driver would have been immersed on farther side, as car kicked boat backward when it started for shore.

Stuck in sand 10 miles beyond the ferry. Broke gear pinion. Camped there [two days] trying to fix car. All grub gone but sardines and one cracker....Cowboy appeared at camp. Sent him to ranger station to telephone Fredonia for relief. Buckboard and horses appeared. Abandoned car.[1]

Traffic was usually light. At intervals, many days would pass without a single traveler wanting to cross the river. Coconino County nevertheless maintained a strong interest in keeping the ferry in operation, since it provided the only direct link with a big portion of the county as well as with the state of Utah.

During this period the ferry operators were still members of the

The "Louse House," where travelers, probably reluctantly, slept at Lee's Ferry. At right is a ramada used for sun shade. *Courtesy Dock Marston, San Francisco*

Johnson family, principally brothers Jerry, Frank, and Price, who all lived at the ranch. Most of their income was derived from the ranch and not from the meager revenue incident to the infrequent ferryboat operation.

County officials wanted to improve the roads on either side of Lee's Ferry, but they were faced with the difficult fact that the ferry itself would still be the weakest part of the road system. Every few years a serious accident occurred at the ferry. Frequently men drowned. Often an accident would take the ferry out of service for days or even months.

In July 1923, for instance, an accident occurred when the rear pulley on the track cable jammed, throwing the boat out of control. On board at the time were two women, three men, and six boys. The ferryman yelled at the passengers to get into the small canoe that was being towed behind the ferryboat. Yet the canoe could not hold them all. At that point Irving G. Cockroft, resident engineer at the water gauging station, saw the emergency and quickly launched his tiny skiff. Cockroft was able to pull some of the people out of the water into the canoe, and he helped others find hand-holds. Then they worked their way toward shore, paddling and swimming, but were carried by the current more than a mile before they reached land. Just as they climbed out they saw the ferryboat capsize, spilling two automobiles and other gear into the river. Cockroft had to go rescue the ferryman, who had been left hanging

80

In June 1928, the ferryboat capsized with three men and a Model T Ford aboard. All the men were drowned and the boat was lost. Since Navajo Bridge was then under construction, the ferryboat was never replaced. *Courtesy Museum of Northern Arizona*

by his hands on the cable. Fortunately no one was drowned, but ferry service was discontinued until the equipment could be repaired or rebuilt.[2]

By this time almost everyone realized that the only acceptable alternative to periodic accidents like this one was to build a bridge. Bridging Marble Canyon had been contemplated even before the ferry began operations in 1873. In 1870, Major John Wesley Powell was reported to have found a place—perhaps Marble Canyon—where a suspension bridge for a railroad could be built.[3] In 1881 the Arizona Northern Railway Company, which was associated with the Denver and Rio Grande Western Railway, had its engineers examine possible bridge sites near Lee's Ferry. A site was selected and approaches were graded before the work was suspended. The projected rail line, of course, was never built.[4]

By the 1920s, when new highways were being built across the United States, a fast, reliable road link between Arizona and Utah was given high priority, but funds were not easily found. Finally, the U.S. Bureau of Indian Affairs pledged $100,000 to build a bridge that would connect the Navajo Reservation with country to the north. The State of Arizona agreed to pay the remainder, or about $300,000.[5]

Although the original plan called for a suspension bridge, it was redesigned as a steel arch bridge that would be anchored to the canyon wall. Work began in June 1927, at a point about six miles downstream from Lee's Ferry. The site was near but was not identical to the place

81

selected by the Rio Grande Railroad surveyors forty-six years earlier.[6]

Due to its isolation and the rugged terrain, the logistics of bridge construction were a constant problem. To transport the heavy steel and other material from Flagstaff required traversing one hundred and thirty miles of almost totally unimproved road which led through sand washes, up and down steep grades, and over rolling and uneven rocky hills. Construction crews completed the job in phases, working first on one side of the canyon, then crossing at Lee's Ferry with their tools and material to work on the other side. Many such ferry crossings were necessary.

Heavy trucks and even heavier loads of bridge steel caused considerable strain on the ferryboat, on the track cable, and on the attaching cables and pulleys. As stated in a 1929 issue of *Arizona Highways*, "This ferry boat, in all probability, would have lived its alloted three score years and ten and now be resting peacefully in some museum instead of on the bottom of the river if the construction of the new bridge had not thrown extra burdens upon the already decrepit ship."[7]

The end came on June 7, 1928. With spring runoff swelling the river, the flow was measured at 85,600 cubic feet of water per second—only a moderately high flow, yet dangerous to an already weakened ferryboat and cable system. On that day a trader named Royce Dean, with a Navajo passenger, Lewis Nez, drove a Model T Ford onto the boat from the north shore. Dean and his companion were returning from Kanab, where they had been trading, to Cedar Ridge, Arizona, their home base.

Jerry Johnson, the regular ferryman, was away working on the bridge construction. In his place was his young nephew, Adolph Johnson. With his two passengers and the Model T on board, Adolph set the cables and started across the river. When the boat touched the south shore, Johnson jumped out and attempted to snub the bow line to a post. Before he could tie the rope, however, the boat began to drift upstream, caught in an unusual eddy current caused by the high river flow. Johnson dug in his heels and tried to hold the boat, but he was dragged down the slope and into the water. He swam to the boat and climbed aboard.

By this time the boat was drifting upstream under its track cable. Attaching cables became slack. Then the eddy current pushed the boat further out into the river where it was caught by the fast downstream flow. Johnson could not work quickly enough adjusting the cables to angle the craft properly to the current. Reaching the end of the slack, the boat nosed under and began taking water. Within a few moments it capsized and the track cable snapped. All three men were drowned. Young Johnson's wife was watching from shore.

An attempt was made to save the boat, which had hung up on the bank some distance below the ferry site. No one could reach it, however, before it drifted on down into Marble Canyon.[8] This accident was the worst ever to happen at Lee's Ferry. It was also the final run of the ferry. For fifty-five years, ferryboats had traveled back and forth across the muddy Colorado at Lee's Ferry. Now they would cross no more. An era of pioneering had come to an end.

Since the new bridge was nearing completion, county officials declined to spend the funds necessary to put the ferry back into operation. Thus from June 1928 to January 1929, highway travelers could not cross the river anywhere between Moab, Utah, and points below the Grand Canyon. When the bridge contractor had to move equipment or materials to the other side of the canyon, he had to send his trucks on a circuitous eight hundred-mile trip through Needles, California—to a destination only eight hundred feet from the starting point![9]

Another spectacular accident occurred at the bridge itself a week after the ferry accident when an ironworker named Lafe McDaniels lost his footing and fell four hundred sixty feet to the Colorado River.[10] No net was being used for fear that hot rivets might start a fire. As it was, McDaniels was the only workman killed during the construction.

In spite of difficulties, work progressed on schedule through the closing of the steel arch, installation of vertical piers, and placement of the concrete deck. On January 12, 1929, the bridge was opened to traffic.

In what the *Coconino Sun* in Flagstaff headlined as the "Biggest News in Southwest History," the new bridge was dedicated on June 14 and 15, 1929. Governors of Arizona, Utah, New Mexico, and Nevada,

The two arching segments of Navajo Bridge approach a union 467 feet above the river in Marble Canyon. The bridge opened to traffic in 1929. *Courtesy U.S. Geological Survey*

and Mormon Church President Heber J. Grant made speeches. Since it was still the time of prohibition, a bottle of *ginger ale* was used to christen the bridge. In spite of the bad roads, an almost incredible crowd of seven thousand was on hand. The Flagstaff newspaper added that two thousand Indians were also present.[11] Indian dances were held in the evening. For many spectators, however, the biggest thrill came when Jack Irish of Flagstaff flew his airplane, an American Eagle 110, down the canyon and under the bridge.

All during construction, and even through the dedication, the bridge was called the Grand Canyon Bridge. Many people in northern Arizona, however, wanted to commemorate the old ferry by calling it "Lee's Ferry Bridge," and a bill to this effect was introduced in the Arizona legislature. Opposition to the bill was not long in coming. Notified of the bill to name it Lee's Ferry Bridge, Mormon President Heber J. Grant wrote to the Arizona State Historian, "I think it would be an outrage on the Mormon people, who were among the first and most substantial settlers of Arizona, to have this bridge named the Lee Bridge."[12] At that time Grant and the other church authorities still believed Lee to be almost solely responsible for the Mountain Meadows Massacre.

President Grant carried his appeal directly to the Arizona legislature, addressing them in person. He suggested that the bridge be named Hamblin Bridge, for Jacob Hamblin, or "Hamblin-Hastele Bridge," for both Hamblin and Navajo Chief Hastele, who had been a friend to the Mormons.[13]

None of the suggested names, however, could avoid factional argument. As a compromise, an amendment was finally submitted to the effect that the bridge be called Navajo Bridge, a non-controversial name that was adopted.

16   GATEWAY TO THE CANYONS

Major Powell was the first to discover how useful Lee's Ferry could be as an access point to the Colorado, for it enabled him to break his second voyage into two segments. Then came Robert B. Stanton, with his railroad surveys in 1889 and 1890, who found Lee's Ferry indispensable as a supply point. While Powell and Stanton embodied the roles of explorer, scientist, and engineer, a new breed of river boatmen appeared in 1896.

In that year George F. Flavell and Ramon Montez passed by Lee's Ferry on their way through the Colorado River's principal canyons. They were followed the next year by Nathaniel T. Galloway and William Richmond. Although Galloway and Richmond did some trapping, both teams ran the Colorado primarily for sport, the first to do so.[1]

Few would follow, however, until a number of articles and books appeared that publicized the adventure awaiting a canyon voyager. Noteworthy were the books of Frederick S. Dellenbaugh, who, in *A Canyon Voyage* (1908), wrote a somewhat exaggerated account of his experiences with Major Powell on the 1871-72 voyage. Another influential book was Ellsworth L. Kolb's *Through the Grand Canyon from Wyoming to Mexico* (1914), which was a detailed and accurate account of the moviemaking trip Ellsworth and his brother Emery made in 1911-12.

Even with the publicity the sport took hold slowly. It was difficult to reach the river from large cities, few guides were available, adequate maps were non-existent until the 1920s, and navigational techniques as well as boat designs had not advanced far enough to insure anything but a hazardous, uncertain ride through the rapids. During the first decade of the twentieth century, only three trips were made through the Grand Canyon. One took place in 1912, two in the 1920s, four in the 1930s, and

With military precision, tents to house visitors are staked behind the Lee's Ferry Fort for the 1935 reunion of pioneers and their descendants who had crossed at Lee's Ferry to settle in Arizona. *Courtesy U.S. Geological Survey, Tucson*

six in the 1940s. Many of these trips, especially the later ones, used Lee's Ferry as a starting point.[2]

Norman D. Nevills was the first to undertake commercial boating through these canyons for paying passengers. Nevills first reached Lee's Ferry in 1936. In 1940, on his first trip past Lee's Ferry and on through the Grand Canyon, one of his passengers was the future U.S. Senator from Arizona, Barry Goldwater. Goldwater's interest in these canyons, and in Colorado River history, continues strong to this day.

Glen Canyon, which lies upstream from Lee's Ferry, was not initially

A passenger on an early commercial river trip was Barry Goldwater, later to become U.S. Senator from Arizona. In this 1940 photograph he appears to be operating a short term—and obviously small scale—laundry service along the river bank. *Courtesy Arizona Historical Foundation*

popular for boating because the early sporting emphasis was on running rapids, of which Glen Canyon had none of any consequence. With but a few exceptions, most travelers noticed little of Glen Canyon's beauty and only expressed impatience at the slow, meandering current. It was not until after World War II that the expanded use of color photography made people see the dazzling spectrum of sunlight and shadow in this intricate sandstone gorge.

In Glen Canyon some of the first paying passengers were customers of Art Greene, who began making occasional boat trips from Lee's Ferry to Aztec Creek, the access point for Rainbow Bridge. Greene had boated on the San Juan River and was well acquainted with the canyon country and the Navajo Reservation. In 1943 he became manager of Marble Canyon Lodge (at Navajo Bridge) and soon thereafter began his sporadic tours to Rainbow Bridge.[3]

Greene's early trips were made in a tiny, thirteen-foot rowboat powered by a twenty horsepower outboard. After the war he increased the size and the number of his boats, but he kept his operations simple. If a motor developed bad trouble he simply drifted back to Lee's Ferry. Whenever he chanced upon another river runner, all of whom were well-known to Greene and his family, it was common to make camp then and there, so that the friends could "swap lies." Schedules were almost non-existent. Art just told his customers that he would take them to Rainbow Bridge and back and that it would take "up to a week."

To avoid trouble caused by hidden sandbars and rocks, Greene experimented with an air-driven boat powered by an airplane engine and propeller mounted on the top deck. After trying a few smaller engines he finally settled on a huge 450-horsepower Pratt & Whitney "Duster" engine that he put on the boat in 1952.

One big problem was that the engine burned great quantities of gasoline, so much that cans of gasoline had to be placed in advance at certain places beside the river. From the visitor's point of view, however, the major drawback was the terrible noise of the engine. Earplugs and cotton were standard issue to all guests and crew. To communicate while enroute, Art tried a hose with funnels at each end, but that didn't work. He finally gave everyone a pencil and note pad for important messages. As Art "Bill" Greene, Jr. said, "You couldn't hear for a week after one of those trips!"

In spite of its drawbacks, Art's air boat performed beautifully. In very shallow water, for instance, it seemed to rise up on its own "pressure wave." Frequently the boat would lurch slightly and those on board could look back and see grooves cut through a sandbar. In optimum conditions the boat could reach a speed of fifty-five miles an hour. Greene operated the air boat until 1960.

Throughout these years, Greene was also developing general tourist accommodations. Shortly after the war he began building Cliff Dwellers Lodge on U.S. 89a, a few miles from Navajo Bridge. He and his family first constructed the strange cabins under, around, and over some balanced rocks just west of Soap Creek. Later, in the immediate vicinity, he built the modern lodge that is still in use.

From Bureau of Reclamation engineers who stayed at Greene's lodge during the late 1940s and early 1950s, Art learned many details about the Glen Canyon Dam and reservoir. Using this base of knowledge, Art examined much of the shoreline of the future lake by airplane, four-wheel drive vehicle, and horse, until he at last pinpointed the best site for a lodge—on a hillside above Wahweap Creek. Art leased his chosen land first from the State of Arizona and then from the U.S. Government. On this land, now the shore of Lake Powell, stands Wahweap Lodge.

During the 1940s, while Art Greene was running his earlier trips from Lee's Ferry upriver to Rainbow Bridge, Glen Canyon was "discovered" by Boy Scouts and many others. Mostly untrained as boatmen, these people floated the easy waters of the Colorado from Hite, near the head of the canyon, down to Lee's Ferry. Using war surplus neoprene rafts, canoes, kayaks — almost anything that would float — they journeyed through magnificent Glen Canyon. First hundreds, then thousands, made the trip, and all of them left the river at Lee's Ferry. As a result of their traffic through Glen Canyon from 1946 to 1956, Lee's Ferry was visited by far more people that at any other time in its history.

After 1956 boating through the damsite was prohibited, so Glen Canyon voyagers left the river at Kane Creek where a graded road reached the river bank. After this Lee's Ferry faded somewhat from public view, but Art Greene continued to run short trips from Lee's Ferry up to Glen Canyon Dam until 1963. River running through Grand Canyon was becoming a popular sport by 1963 and Lee's Ferry was the starting point for these trips.

Lee's Ferry was included in the lands either acquired or withdrawn for the Glen Canyon National Recreation Area. The only exception was the one hundred sixty-acre homestead at the Lee's Ferry Ranch, which continued as private property until July 1974, when it was purchased by the U.S. Government.

In 1963 the National Park Service moved into Lee's Ferry to establish a recreation site. As an access point to the river the place was essential, since only at Lee's Ferry could tourists and boaters reach the clean, cold tailwater that was discharged from the dam. Short trips could be made upriver through Glen Canyon to the dam. Even more important, however, was that Lee's Ferry was the only launching site for commercial river trips down Marble and Grand Canyons.

To the National Park Service Lee's Ferry was something of an enigma. Its importance as a recreation site was undeniable, yet it was also a

A powerboat cruises past the old ferry site and up into Glen Canyon. Here the fishing is good and the scenery superb.

historic site. Any action to put in boat ramps, motel, store, parking lots, or access roads was likely to interfere with the historical integrity of specific points. Still, Lee's Ferry could not be maintained solely as an open air museum. In the process of development, a few historic points were altered, but mostly because their significance was then poorly understood. Every indication now exists that future development at Lee's Ferry will be undertaken carefully, and then only with full aware-ness of probable consequences to specific historic points.

In 1967 the Fort Lee Company purchased the concession at Lee's Ferry and has been operating it ever since. The owner-manager, Tony Lee Sparks, has initiated a popular daily float trip from Glen Canyon Dam down to Lee's Ferry. Sparks and his employees seem highly aware of the history of the area and have even published brief historical sum-maries, in pamphlet form, for distribution to tourists. Sparks has also entered the business of boating commercially through Marble and Grand Canyons.

White water boating has changed considerably since the early rough and adventurous trips in wooden boats through the Grand Canyon. Of significance has been new boating equipment—first rubber rafts, then eventually twenty-eight-foot long bridge pontoons, often called "baloneys." The switch to motor power greatly changed methods of running the rapids and permitted use of the big baloneys. Some of those who still use wooden boats now float the river in dories—flat bottom boats that curve upward at each end—which can be maneuvered rapidly by a skilled boatman.

Boating downriver from Lee's Ferry grew substantially in volume after Glen Canyon Dam was built. Perhaps the dam construction coincided with a nationwide increase in river boating. Or, as some claim,

From Lee's Ferry, the river plunges into the scenic depths of Marble Canyon then into Grand Canyon. Each year about 16,000 people make a memorable boat trip through these canyons. *Courtesy Bureau of Reclamation*

perhaps the longer boating season permitted by regulation of seasonal flows through the dam led to an increase in Colorado River boating. Undoubtedly, the controversy during the 1960s over whether or not to build Bridge Canyon Dam in lower Grand Canyon stimulated much interest in the river run through Grand Canyon.

Whatever the cause, the number of boaters through the Grand Canyon rose from about two hundred eighty in 1962 to nearly sixteen thousand in 1973. The number of people permitted to make the trip each year is now controlled by the National Park Service.

On a typical day between March and October, one will see all manner of boating tourists, from bikini-clad college girls to grizzled river veterans, from high school boys drinking their first beer to thoughtful retired couples. All find their place at Lee's Ferry and on the Colorado River. Once in the canyons a boating tourist usually discovers that his customary identity has little importance and that he or she becomes one with the crew, with fellow passengers, with the canyon, and with the river.

As a gateway across the river, Lee's Ferry's days ended in 1928, but as a gateway to the Colorado River, Lee's Ferry's days have only just begun.

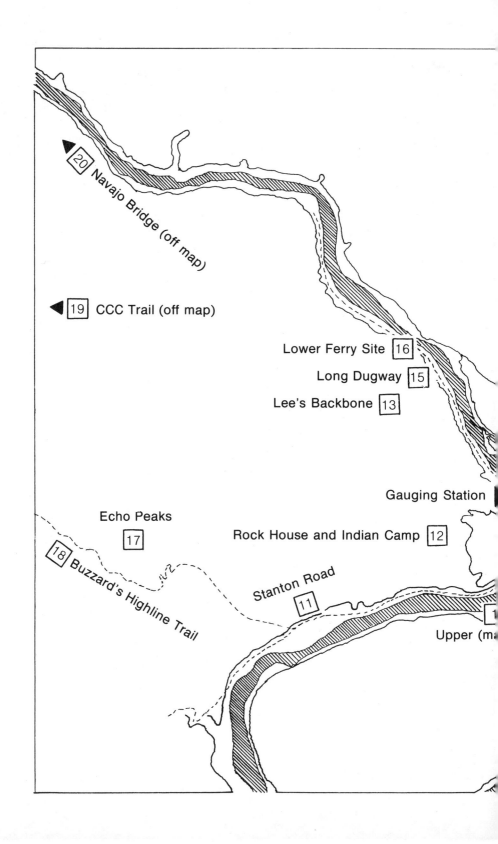

20 Navajo Bridge (off map)

19 CCC Trail (off map)

Lower Ferry Site 16

Long Dugway 15

Lee's Backbone 13

Gauging Station

Echo Peaks

17

18 Buzzard's Highline Trail

Rock House and Indian Camp 12

Stanton Road

11

Upper (m

1

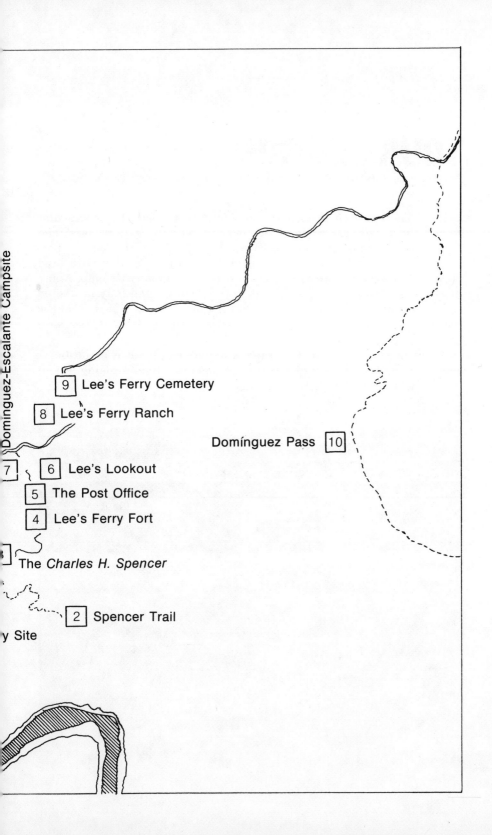

Domínguez-Escalante Campsite

9 Lee's Ferry Cemetery

8 Lee's Ferry Ranch

Domínguez Pass 10

7

6 Lee's Lookout

5 The Post Office

4 Lee's Ferry Fort

The *Charles H. Spencer*

2 Spencer Trail

y Site

TOUR SECTION

A Guide to Historic Sites and Places At and Near Lee's Ferry

Lee's Ferry is rich in visible traces of history, yet the spectacular desert landscape is apt to dominate, even to overawe; historic sites tend to be inconspicuous and need to be pointed out. All of the more important accessible sites are listed in this Tour Section, together with brief sketches. These sites are also shown on the accompanying map. Many sites are clustered near the present Fort Lee store and may be visited within a short time. The National Park Service District Ranger and the concessionaire at the Fort Lee Company are further sources of assistance and directions.

A warning: *None* of the old trails or abandoned roads is maintained, and all have some hazards. A few are dangerous. Before hiking any of them, check with the District Ranger.

The incredible Spencer Trail

1. **Upper (main) Ferry Site.** The most important ferry crossing site was upstream about half a mile from the Fort Lee Company store. Here ferryboats operated continually from 1873 to 1878, during the spring and early summer from 1873 to 1896, and continually from 1896 to 1928. It was at this upper ferry site that most of the early Mormon emigrants from Utah crossed the river as they heeded the "call" to settle in Arizona. Most emigrants considered the river crossing as the one real danger on the long trip (see Chapter 9). In 1896 a heavy track cable was hung across the river at this site to hold the boat. From then until 1928, this site was used throughout the year.

Ferry accidents at the various crossing sites caused drownings in 1876, 1880, 1884, 1899, 1911 and 1928. In the last accident, June 7, 1928, three men drowned. It was a tragic finale to ferry operations at Lee's Ferry. Since Navajo Bridge was then under construction, the ferryboat was never replaced (see Chapter 15). Although little evidence of former activity remains at the upper ferry site, some rock foundations of cabins used by ferrymen and travelers are visible. Nearby is a section of heavy cable used to hold the ferry.

Across the river the old approach road to the ferry, dug out of the steep river bank, leads downstream. The landing on the opposite shore was at the low point in the road. Extending upstream from the ferry site is another dugway, the Stanton Road (see Site No. 11).

2. **Spencer Trail.** The Spencer Trail climbs the steep slope east of the Fort to the Canyon rim, 1500 feet above the river. Switchbacking ingeniously around sheer ledges, the trail even today seems a marvel of engineering. It was built in 1910 by a mining company headed by Charles H. Spencer. One report says that it was laid out, at least in part, by a clever mule named Pete (see Chapter 13). Spencer intended to pack coal by mule train from Warm Creek Canyon over the trail. Although the Spencer Trail was little used for coal transport, for other travelers it was a decided improvement over the Domínguez Pass Trail (see Site No. 10), two and one-half miles up the Paria.

The Spencer Trail is not maintained, but it is still passable to hikers who exercise care and good judgment. Hikers on this historic route are rewarded with magnificent views seldom equalled in the canyon and plateau country of the Colorado River. Before setting out check trail conditions by consulting the National Park Service office.

3. The ***Charles H. Spencer.*** In the mud of the riverbank lies the hulk of a stern paddlewheel steamboat known as the *Charles H. Spencer*. This steamer, twenty-five feet wide and ninety-two feet long, was the largest craft ever floated on the Colorado River above the Grand Canyon. It was built in San Francisco in 1911, dismantled, and shipped by

rail and wagon to the mouth of Warm Creek, in Glen Canyon, where it was reassembled. The company headed by Charles H. Spencer, mining entrepreneur at Lee's Ferry, brought the boat to the Colorado River to haul coal from the Warm Creek mines to Lee's Ferry. The coal was to be used to fire steam boilers for sluicing gold particles from the abundant outcropping of Chinle shale located about two hundred yards north of Lee's Ferry Fort. One of the big steam boilers still remains near the spot where Spencer centered his mining operations.

During 1912, the *Charles H. Spencer* made five one-way trips, ending up at Lee's Ferry. The steamboat was not efficient; it needed almost all the coal it could carry to power its way back upstream to Warm Creek. At any rate, the mining venture failed because of other factors and the coal was not needed (see Chapter 13). The *Charles H. Spencer* remains a visible artifact that illustrates one of the more dramatic chapters in mining along the Colorado River.

Ruin of the *Charles H. Spencer*

4. **Lee's Ferry Fort.** Near the store and parking lot, and quite obvious to visitors, is Lee's Ferry Fort. Built primarily as a trading post—not as a fort—its construction in 1874 was a means of keeping peace between the Navajos of Arizona and the whites of southern Utah.

Trouble erupted in January 1874, when three Navajos were killed and another wounded by white men while the Indians were on a trading trip into south-central Utah. The wounded Navajo, who managed to struggle back to Arizona Territory, precipitated demands for revenge, if not outright war, against the white settlers. The incident threatened to engulf the Mormon–Navajo frontier in further bloodshed, but the situation finally cooled. As a means of keeping Navajos out of southern Utah, the Mormons decided that a post at Lee's Ferry would be helpful. In July 1874, a construction crew from the L.D.S. St. George Stake built the trading post (see Chapter 8).

Lee's Ferry Fort

No evidence exists that the building was ever under attack. It was used only intermittently as a trading post but was used in later years as a residence, a school, and a mess hall.

Note the name "J. Hislop 1889" near the front doorway. John Hislop was with Robert B. Stanton on a railroad survey down the Colorado. Stanton and his men had Christmas dinner beside the fort in 1889 (see Chapter 12).

John D. Lee had no connection with the building or operation of the Lee's Ferry Fort.

5. **Post Office.** The small rock cabin located a short distance west of the fort was used as a post office. An official post office was maintained at Lee's Ferry from 1879 to 1923.

6. **Lee's Lookout.** The round knob of Shinarump conglomerate rising about 175 feet above and northwest of Lee's Ferry Fort is Lee's Lookout. From it can be seen the lower Paria, the Vermilion Cliffs, lower Glen Canyon, and upper Marble Canyon—in fact, the entire Lee's Ferry area.

Unfounded reports that John D. Lee, as a fugitive, actually used the knob for a lookout point led to the present name, but there can be little truth to the reports. In his short time at Lee's Ferry, Lee was far too busy working on the ranch or tending to ferryboat duties to have time for standing around on high ledges.

Atop the knob is a low circle of rocks about twenty feet in diameter. This circle was there before Lee arrived, for a member of the 1869 Powell expedition, Jack Sumner, made a note of it. Still, the origin of the rock circle is a subject of conjecture. Prehistoric Indians may have laid up the stones, but archaeologists have found no evidence to confirm or deny it. The Lookout is an easy hike from the Fort Lee store. Head for the wooden cross posted inside the circle of rocks.

The "standing rock" above the Domínguez-Escalante campsite of 1776

7. **Domínguez–Escalante Campsite.** From October 26 to November 1, 1776, the Spanish padres and their entourage camped on the bank of the Colorado near the mouth of the Paria River. In his diary Escalante reported that the campsite was beside the river near a high rock. They were obviously camped at the base of the Shinarump ridge along the present paved road between the Paria River and Lee's Ferry Fort. Naming their campsite San Benito, the Spaniards gazed at the great cliffs facing them on every side, then with a touch of humor added the name "Salsipuedes," meaning "get out if you can" (see Chapter 3).

In 1869 when a group of Mormon men were sent to the Paria River to guard against marauding Navajos, the Mormons camped under the same rock. They dubbed their small enclosure "Fort Meeks" (see Chapter 4).

Lee's Ferry Ranch house

8. **Lee's Ferry Ranch.** The ranch lies on the nearly flat valley floor within a large meander of the Paria River. Crops and livestock grown here provided economic support for the ferry operators, their families, and others from 1872 to the 1940s. Often the ranch is referred to as "Lonely Dell," which was Emma Lee's description of the entire Lee's Ferry setting when she first saw it in late December 1871.

Although the soil is good, the task of maintaining a constant water supply, particularly in the hot summer months, was often beyond human capability. Flash floods on the Paria repeatedly wiped out diversion dams and either destroyed irrigation ditches or filled them with silt. Work was grueling and virtually unending. When John D. Lee, as a fugitive, left Lee's Ferry to go into hiding, no one remained who was capable of maintaining the irrigation system. Without water in blistering summer heat, Lee's crops soon withered and died. When Lee returned he found all crops dead except a single apricot tree that Emma Lee had hand-watered with a bucket.

After Lee was executed in 1877 and Emma Lee and her children had departed, the new ferry operator, Warren Johnson, built a large, two-story home on the ranch for his two wives and their growing families. Johnson's wooden home lasted through changes in ferry operators until December 1926, when it burned to the ground.

In the 1930s Leo Weaver built the long rock bungalow that still stands on the ranch. It was operated as a dude ranch for some time, but business was poor. The ranch has traded hands a number of times since then. In July 1974, it was purchased by the U.S. Government and is now part of the Glen Canyon National Recreation Area.

On this ranch are a one-room cabin and a log shed, both supposedly built by John D. Lee. One of the Johnson boys, born at Lee's Ferry in 1878, recalls that the two structures were almost certainly there when he was born. In later years the one-room cabin was used as a school house.

9. **Lee's Ferry Cemetery.** Located about one-quarter mile northwest of Lee's Ferry Ranch, the cemetery contains possibly twenty graves, the oldest dated 1874 and the latest dated 1928. Over half of the graves are either poorly marked or bear no marking at all. The earliest grave, that of James Jackson who died in March 1874, is marked only by a pile of loose stones. Among the tragic deaths were four children of ferryman Warren M. Johnson who contacted diphtheria from a passing traveler and died within a period of four weeks during May and June 1891 (see Chapter 11).

10. **Domínguez Pass.** This pass and the steep trail up to it were discovered by the Domínguez-Escalante expedition in 1776. After spending a futile week at San Benito Salsipuedes (Lee's Ferry) trying to cross the Colorado, the priests and their men located this pass. They apparently blazed a new trail from the Paria River up to the pass (see Chapter 3).

Mormon missionaries enroute to the Hopi villages in 1858, 1859, and 1860 also used this route. John D. Lee and others of his day traveled it often, while in later years cowboys, outlaws, and miners occasionally traversed the trail.

100

Today this historic trail across the Echo Cliffs is unmarked and all but forgotten. The trail is traceable only in part, but the entire route is generally apparent. It begins beside the Paria River about two and one-half miles above Lee's Ferry, winds through bleak hills of Chinle shale, then up long slopes of shifting sand, angling southeastward toward a low point in the cliffs—Domínguez Pass. The pass is some two thousand feet above the Paria River.

The Domínguez Pass route can be followed today by well prepared hikers willing to exert strenuous effort and carry ample water. Midway up, the trail crosses a long, steep pitch of soft sand, while near the crest it is extremely steep and angles across narrow sandstone ledges. Anyone planning to make the hike should notify the Park Ranger at Lee's Ferry.

The trail to Domínguez Pass

11. **Stanton Road.** On the south (left) bank of the Colorado River, extending upstream from the upper ferry site about one and one-half miles, is the Stanton Road. It terminates just below the first big bend of the river. This road was put in during 1899 by Robert B. Stanton, railroad promoter turned mining engineer. At the time Stanton was preparing to place a huge gold dredge on the Colorado in upper Glen Canyon. Confident that the dredge would successfully extract gold particles from the river sands, Stanton staked mining claims up and down both sides of the river. The "road" at Lee's Ferry was simply assessment work required to keep some of these claims valid. Stanton's dredge was big and expensive, but it was incapable of capturing the flour-fine gold from the river bed. The entire enterprise soon collapsed (see Chapter 12).

12. **Rock House and Indian Camp.** Located at the base of an alternate wagon road around Lee's Backbone, an abandoned one-room rock house stands beneath the cliffs. Although the origin and purpose of this house have not been determined, it has been used as a camp by Navajo Indians, who have also built a number of small stone corrals nearby. At Lee's Ferry, all of the area south of the river is part of the Navajo Reservation, and the river bottom land is frequently used by these Indians as grazing land for their animals.

Located on the flat near the base of Lee's Backbone (see Site No. 13), is an old paddlewheel. Originally this was attached to the *Navajo,* a scow or barge used by the Southern California Edison Company during their dam site investigations in Glen Canyon from 1921 to 1923.

13. **Lee's Backbone.** What was known as Lee's Backbone is the relatively flat but steeply inclined surface of Shinarump conglomerate on the south side of the river. Over this rock surface, Mormon emigrants took their wagons south from the ferry crossing. It was used continually from 1873 to 1878, when the lower ferry site and dugway were constructed for use during periods of low river flow (see Site No. 16). Still in use during times of high river flow, the Backbone was partially bypassed by a slightly better road over high terrain in 1888. In 1898, when the long dugway was opened (see Site No. 15), Lee's Backbone was completely abandoned.

Lee's Backbone is covered by numerous rock gullies and boulders that brutally pounded wooden wagons and straining animals. Some travelers claimed it was the worst piece of land ever crossed by wagons (see Chapter 9).

Today hikers may follow the old wagon road over Lee's Backbone. In places, grooved wagon ruts can be seen in solid rock. At its highest point, where the road ran literally on the edge of the cliff, evidence of much road work can still be seen. At the extreme southwest end, the road switchbacked down some four hundred feet over a steep talus slope to the fairly level terrain of the Marble Platform.

Lee's Backbone (center)—the first wagon road out of Lee's Ferry to the south

The alternate route, built in 1888 over higher terrain, was not much of an improvement. This bypass can be followed only with difficulty today since much of it has been washed out.

14. **Gauging Station.** Operated by the U.S. Geological Survey, the essential structure of the station is the narrow concrete water recorder well beside the river at the base of Lee's Backbone. This gauging station is the most important one on the entire Colorado River, since it measures the amount of water passing from the Upper to the Lower Basins in fulfillment of the 1922 Colorado River Compact—the "law of the river." The dividing or "Compact" point between the basins is set at one mile below the mouth of the Paria.

One reason for building Glen Canyon Dam was to provide a huge storage reservoir (Lake Powell) that could be used to meet downstream commitments. Whether or not these commitments are met is determined by measurements taken at the Lee's Ferry Gauging Station.

On Grand Canyon river maps the gauging station is marked Mile Zero, the reference point from which distances downstream are measured (see Chapter 14).

15. **Long Dugway.** The long dugway on the south side of the Colorado was built in 1898 so that travelers could bypass the arduous route over Lee's Backbone. Carved from the soft, brown Moenkopi formation, the road follows the contour of the slope and ascends about three hundred feet in a mile. For thirty years it carried all the traffic to and from the upper ferry site—horses, mules, bull teams and wagons, and finally early-day automobiles (see Chapter 11).

Although it is now greatly eroded away, the dugway, when in use, was kept wide enough for one wagon or automobile. But it was none too wide. Sharlot Hall, Arizona State Historian, who traveled this dugway by wagon in 1911, wrote of it, "The road looked as if it had been cut out of the red clay with a pocket knife. Sometimes it hung out over the river so we seemed sliding into the muddy current and again the cliffs above hung over till one grew dizzy to look."

The dugway is boldly visible from a number of points on the north side of the river. Hikers, using care at places where washouts have occurred, may walk the entire dugway.

The Dugway—main road into Lee's Ferry from the south from 1898 to 1928

16. **Lower Ferry Site.** Ferryboats crossed the river at this lower site during low flow stages of the river from 1878 to 1896. The advantage of crossing here was that the road over Lee's Backbone was avoided; on the south side wagons had only to climb the short dugway out of the inner

A short dugway from the Lower Ferry site, used from 1878 to 1896

canyon to strike the main road to the Arizona settlements. This crossing was used each year between August and May. During the spring high water made a crossing here dangerous, if not impossible, so travelers had to use the upper ferry site and had to cross Lee's Backbone. After 1896, when the ferry was finally anchored to a track cable at the upper site, this lower site was abandoned.

The short, steep dugway on the left side of the river at this site may be seen from the campground and from a number of points on the north side of the Colorado.

17. **Echo Peaks.** Across the river to the south rising 2500 feet above Lee's Ferry, the jagged Echo Peaks dominate the horizon. In October 1871, some of Major Powell's men climbed the peaks, and, for amusement, shot a pistol at the river, far below. The sharp report was followed by a twenty-four-second silence, then came the echoes, as "the sound waves were hurled back...with a rattle like that of musketry" (see Chapter 5).

On a warm day in June 1974, W. L. Rusho climbed the peaks and attempted to duplicate the long-delayed echo by firing an 1860 model cap and ball revolver, but without success. Apparently fairly low air temperatures and an absence of wind are necessary to obtain the echo effect described by Powell's men.

The Echo Peaks are the high point in the seventy-five-mile line of

Echo Cliffs extending from Lee's Ferry south almost to Tuba City, nearly paralleling U.S. 89. The cliffs also extend north of the Colorado along the east side of the Paria River canyon.

18. **Buzzard's Highline Trail.** An important Indian trail once descended the Echo Cliffs through rough, broken terrain on the south and east sides of the Echo Peaks, then down a long sand slope to the river. It was reportedly part of a major system of Indian trading trails and may have been used for centuries.

Where a northbound traveler on this trail crosses the ridge and obtains his first view of Lee's Ferry, there he will see a large pile of stones. Many years ago a battle was reported to have occurred here between Navajo and Ute Indians. Subsequently every Navajo who passed threw a rock onto the pile.

Buzzard's Highline Trail

This difficult trail was used on occasion by white men coming into Lee's Ferry from points east. For instance, mining man Charles H. Spencer and some of his men were guided over the trail in May 1910 by a Navajo Indian. It was one of Spencer's men who suggested the name Buzzard's Highline Trail.

Except for a small section near the high ridge overlooking Lee's Ferry, the Buzzard's Highline Trail is extremely faint and difficult to follow. In

106

summer the terrain is oppressively—even dangerously—hot and arid. Consequently, the trail is not recommended for hikers.

Monument to an Indian battle

19. **CCC Trail.** Cresting the Echo Cliffs southwest of the Echo Peaks is the so-called CCC Trail, which was reportedly constructed by Civilian Conservation Corps workmen during the 1930s. A CCC camp definitely did operate in House Rock Valley for some time, but records of that camp have not yet been located. The CCC Trail was apparently built so that Navajo Indians could more easily take their livestock to the river and bottom lands at Lee's Ferry. It was probably a replacement for the Buzzard's Highline Trail (see Site No. 18).

A traveler approaching the river from the south on the CCC Trail crosses the ridge at the head of a side canyon, then switchbacks down talus slopes to the Shinarump ledge. From there, he may traverse across

CCC Trail

to Lee's Backbone or he may descend further to the level of the Marble Platform.

The CCC Trail is an easy hike, but the access road from U.S. 89a to the base of the trail is suitable for four-wheel drive vehicles only. In the vicinity of the base of the trail are numerous uranium prospecting roads and test pits.

20. **Navajo Bridge.** Although located six miles downstream from Lee's Ferry, Navajo Bridge represents a vital part of Lee's Ferry history. In 1928, during construction of the bridge, the ferryboat was lost in a tragic accident (see Site No. 1). The boat was not replaced because completion of the bridge would put the ferry out of operation.

Work began in June 1927 and was completed January 12, 1929, when the bridge was opened to traffic. It was dedicated in June 1929. A proposal to name it "Lee's Ferry Bridge" led to a spirited controversy in the Arizona State Legislature. The name "Navajo Bridge" was the result of compromise.

Until the highway bridge at Glen Canyon Dam site was completed in 1959, Navajo Bridge was the only bridge crossing of the Colorado from Moab, Utah, to Hoover Dam, a distance of almost six hundred miles (see Chapter 15 for further details).

108

Navajo Bridge

READING LIST
A Short List of Books and Articles that Touch on Lee's Ferry

Although several books and articles mention Lee's Ferry, the book you are reading is the first to trace the basic historical facts of this important crossroads. Many events that relate to Lee's Ferry, however, have been discussed more fully in other published books and articles. If not still in print these titles may be found in any good-sized library or university collection.

Two books by C. Gregory Crampton, *Standing Up Country, the Canyon Lands of Utah and Arizona* and *Land of Living Rock, the Grand Canyon and the High Plateaus, Arizona, Utah, Nevada* (New York: Alfred A. Knopf, 1964 and 1972 respectively), place Lee's Ferry in its regional setting and in historical perspective. W. L. Rusho's "Living History at Lee's Ferry," *Journal of the West* 7 (January 1968): 64-75, describes the many reminders of the ferry's rich history. Edwin Corle's *Listen Bright Angel* (New York: Duell, Sloan & Pearce, 1946) is entertaining but somewhat inaccurate. A more authoritative book by J. Donald Hughes, *The Story of Man at Grand Canyon* (Grand Canyon: Grand Canyon Natural History Association, 1967), touches a wide area but concentrates on the National Park. Works by F. S. Dellenbaugh, *The Romance of the Colorado River* (New York and London: G. P. Putnam's Sons, 1902), Lewis R. Freeman, *The Colorado River, Yesterday, To-Day, and To-Morrow* (New York: Dodd, Mead & Co., 1923), and Frank Waters, *The Colorado* (New York: Rinehart & Co., 1946) treat Lee's Ferry briefly in the perspective of Colorado River history.

On local geology, a report by David A. Phoenix, *Geology of the Lee's Ferry Area, Coconino County, Arizona* (Washington: Government Printing Office, 1963), U.S. Geological Survey Bulletin 1137, emphasizes stratigraphy. Theodore Roosevelt's description of the Vermilion Cliffs is in his article about his pack trip, "Across the Navajo Desert," *Outlook* 105 (October 1913).

Abundant technical literature can be found on the prehistoric Indian cultures of the canyon country, but no archaeological study has yet concentrated on Lee's Ferry and its environs. In an article entitled "The Canyon Dwellers," *The American West* 4 (May 1967), Robert C. Euler discusses the split twig figurines and the prehistoric life in the Colorado River canyons. Evidence of the Desha Complex found near Navajo Mountain is in Alexander J. Lindsay, Jr. et al, *Survey and Excavations North and East of Navajo Mountain, Utah, 1959-1962* (Flagstaff: Museum of Northern Arizona, 1968), Bulletin No. 45, Glen Canyon Series No. 8. A summary of successive Indian cultures is found in Robert C. Euler, *Southern Paiute Ethnohistory*, (Salt Lake City: University of Utah, 1966), Anthropological Papers 78, Glen Canyon Series 28. Navajo history and expansion are covered by James J. Hester, *Early Navajo Migrations and Acculturation in the Southwest* (Santa Fe: Museum of New Mexico, 1962),

111

Papers in Anthropology 6. The historical importance of the Navajo trader is detailed by Frank McNitt, *The Indian Trader* (Norman: University of Oklahoma Press, 1962).

Concerning the Domínguez-Escalante Expedition, Herbert E. Bolton, "Pageant in the Wilderness," *Utah Historical Quarterly* 18 (1950), has the best interpretation of the route followed by the Spanish padres. What appears to be a superior translation of Escalante's diary, however, was published as Herbert S. Auerbach, "Father Escalante's Journal, 1776-77," *Utah Historical Quarterly* 11 (1943). A new translation by Fray Angelico Chavez will be published by the Utah Historical Society in the near future.

The mountain men who trapped the Colorado River canyons left few records, and only scattered references to their activities are extant. The overland caravan trade between Santa Fe and Los Angeles is summarized in LeRoy R. and Ann W. Hafen, *The Old Spanish Trail, Santa Fe to Los Angeles, with Extracts from Contemporary Records, and Including Diaries of Antonio Armijo and Orville Pratt* (Glendale, California: Arthur H. Clark Co., 1954).

Early Mormon explorations and expeditions to the Indian country across the Colorado are narrated in an autobiographical account by Jacob Hamblin, taken down by James A. Little, entitled *Jacob Hamblin Among the Indians* (Salt Lake City: Juvenile Instructor Office, 1881). Two biographies: Pearson H. Corbett, *Jacob Hamblin, the Peacemaker* (Salt Lake City: Deseret Book Co., 1952), and Paul Bailey, *Jacob Hamblin, Buckskin Apostle* (Los Angeles: Westernlore Press, 1948), give the noted explorer a stature bordering on the heroic.

John Wesley Powell's voyage down the Colorado River and his attendant land explorations are surely the most written-about episodes in Colorado River history. Lee's Ferry and environs figure prominently in Powell's second expedition of 1871-72, reported in detail by one of the members, Frederick S. Dellenbaugh in *A Canyon Voyage* (New Haven: Yale University Press, 1962). A number of diaries kept by members of Powell's first and second expeditions were published in special issues of the *Utah Historical Quarterly,* 1947-1949. Some of these diaries were edited by W. C. Darrah, whose biography *Powell of the Colorado* (Princeton: Princeton University Press, 1951), is a standard work. An excellent broad treatment of Powell's role in western history is Wallace Stegner, *Beyond the Hundredth Meridian* (Cambridge, Mass.: Riverside Press, 1954).

The Mountain Meadows Massacre, 2nd ed. (Norman: University of Oklahoma Press, 1962), and *John Doyle Lee, Zealot-Pioneer-Scapegoat* (Glendale, Calif.: Arthur H. Clark Co., 1962) are balanced and scholarly books by Juanita Brooks. Especially valuable for Lee's activities at Lee's Ferry is Robert G. Cleland and Juanita Brooks, eds., *A Mormon Chronicle, the Diaries of John D. Lee, 1848-1876,* (San Marino, Calif.: Huntington Library, 1955).

The history and early use of Lee's Ferry by Mormons, as well as the colonization of the Little Colorado River country may be found in James H. McClintock, *Mormon Settlement in Arizona: A Record of Peaceful Conquest of the Desert* (Phoenix: Manufacturing Stationers, 1921). A highly readable, scholarly work based on original documents is Charles S. Peterson, *Take Up Your Mission: Mormon Colonizing Along the Little Colorado River, 1870-1890* (Tucson: University of Arizona Press, 1973). A valuable article on the role of Warren M. Johnson at Lee's Ferry was written by P. T. Reilly as "Warren Marshall Johnson, Forgotten Saint," *Utah Historical Quarterly* 39 (Winter 1971): 3-22.

Probably the best account of the 1874 shooting of Navajos in Grass Valley appeared in Peter Gottfredson, *History of Indian Depredations in Utah* (Salt Lake City: Skelton Publishing Co., 1919): 330-332.

Only a few scattered references are found concerning visits of outlaws to the Lee's Ferry country. Matt Warners' autobiography was entitled *The Last of the Bandit Riders* (New York: Bonanza Books, 1940). Ralph Keithley, in *Buckey O'Neill* (Caldwell, Idaho: Caxton Printers, 1949), details the exploits of one of Arizona's most colorful lawmen.

Robert B. Stanton's own writings are in Robert B. Stanton, *Down the Colorado,* ed. by Dwight L. Smith (Norman: University of Oklahoma Press, 1965), the dramatic story of the railroad survey through the Colorado River canyons. Stanton's record of his mining venture in Glen Canyon has been edited by C. Gregory Crampton and Dwight L. Smith, *The Hoskaninni Papers: Mining in Glen Canyon, 1897-1902* (Salt Lake City: University of Utah, 1961), Anthropological Papers 54. Less has been written about mining entrepreneur Charles H. Spencer. The only article to appear so far was W. L. Rusho, "Charlie Spencer's Wonderful Steamboat," *Arizona Highways* 37 (August 1962).

Zane Grey has portrayed Buffalo Jones in *Last of the Plainsmen* (New York: Outing Publishing Co., 1908), and James Emett in "The Man Who Influenced Me Most," *American* 102 (August 1926), and in *Tales of Lonely Trails* (New York and London: Harper and Bros., 1922). More detail on Buffalo Jones and on the "cattalo" experiment in House Rock Valley is in Robert Easton and Mackensie Brown, *Lord of Beasts: the Saga of Buffalo Jones* (Tucson: University of Arizona Press, 1961). A colorful description of the Lee's Ferry country in the early twentieth century is Sharlot M. Hall, *Sharlot Hall on the Arizona Strip: A Diary of a Journey Through Northern Arizona in 1911,* ed. by C. Gregory Crampton (Flagstaff: Northland Press, 1975).

The merits of building a dam in lower Glen Canyon were first discussed by Lewis R. Freeman in *The Colorado River, Yesterday, To-Day, and To-Morrow* (New York: Dodd, Mead and Co., 1923). In *The Colorado* (New York and Toronto: Rinehart & Co., 1946), author Frank Waters reviews the history of dam construction on the Colorado up to that time.

Although a substantial literature now exists on running the Colorado, almost all writers provide only glimpses of life at Lee's Ferry. Otis "Dock" Marston in "River Runners: Fast Water Navigation," *Utah Historical Quarterly* 28 (July 1960), lists the Green and Colorado River boating parties through Utah after the Powell expeditions. The Kolb brothers ran the Colorado in 1911 and provided a good picture of Spencer's operations at Lee's Ferry and at Warm Creek. See Ellsworth L. Kolb, *Through the Grand Canyon from Wyoming to Mexico* (New York: Macmillan Co., 1914). Barry M. Goldwater, who made the Colorado run in 1940 with Norman Nevills, provides a short history of Lee's Ferry as well as valuable personal observations in his *Delightful Journey Down the Green & Colorado Rivers* (Tempe, Arizona: Arizona Historical Foundation, 1970). Art Greene was the subject of a brief biography by Frank Jensen, "Riverman," *Desert Magazine* (July 1962). Other references to Greene and his river operations have appeared in numerous regional travel magazines and in newspapers.

Administration of Lee's Ferry as part of the Glen Canyon National Recreation Area is too recent to have received much publicity.

FOOTNOTES

1   A POINT OF VIEW

1. In *Sixth Report of the United States Geographic Board: 1890 to 1932* (Washington: Government Printing Office, 1933) the name was decreed to be Lees Ferry (not Lee nor Lee's). Such a decision, however, is both poor grammar and poor history, since no person named Lees was ever involved. Hence, the authors consistently insert an apostrophe in Lee's Ferry.

2. The geology of the Lee's Ferry area is included in Herbert E. Gregory and Raymond C. Moore, *The Kaiparowits Region: A Geographic and Geologic Reconnaissance of Parts of Utah and Arizona* (Washington: Government Printing Office, 1931) U.S. Geological Survey, and in Charles B. Hunt, *Cenozoic Geology of the Colorado Plateau* (Washington: Government Printing Office, 1956) U.S. Geological Survey, and in Charles B. Hunt, "Geologic History of the Colorado River," *The Colorado River Region and John Wesley Powell* (Washington: Government Printing Office, 1969) U.S. Geological Survey Professional Paper 669. In David A. Phoenix, *Geology of The Lees Ferry Area, Coconino County, Arizona* (Washington: Government Printing Office, 1963) U.S. Geological Survey, the emphasis is on stratigraphy and possible deposits of uranium ore.

3. Theodore Roosevelt, "Across the Navajo Desert," *Outlook* 105 (October 1913).

2   THE FIRST MEN

1. Split twig figurines and prehistoric life in the Colorado River canyons are discussed in Robert C. Euler, "The Canyon Dwellers," *The American West* 4 (May 1967). The succession of Indian cultures is treated in Robert C. Euler, *Southern Paiute Ethnohistory* (Salt Lake City: University of Utah, 1966) Anthropological Papers No. 78, Glen Canyon Series No. 28.

2. The Desha Complex is discussed in Alexander J. Lindsay, Jr. et al, *Survey and Excavations North and East of Navajo Mountain, Utah, 1959-1962* (Flagstaff: Museum of Northern Arizona, 1968) Bulletin No. 45, Glen Canyon Series No. 8.

3. *Arizona Daily Sun* (Flagstaff), 24 July 1963, article by William Hoyt.

4. James J. Hester, *Early Navajo Migrations and Acculturation in the Southwest* (Santa Fe: Museum of New Mexico, 1962) Papers in Anthropology No. 6.

3   THROUGH AN UNKNOWN LAND

1. Three major translations of the Escalante diary have been made. The first, W. R. Harris, *The Catholic Church in Utah, 1776-1909* (Salt Lake City: Intermountain Catholic Press, 1909), was a loose translation that generalized details. Probably the most accurate translation was Herbert S. Auerbach, "Father Escalante's Journal, 1776-77," *Utah Historical Quarterly* 11 (1943). The only interpretive study that attempted to relate the Escalante narrative to present-day topographic names was Herbert E. Bolton, "Pageant in the Wilderness," *Utah Historical Quarterly* 18 (1950). All names supplied by the Spaniards were put on a map prepared by expedition cartographer Captain Bernardo Miera y Pacheco. Miera's was the first map to show a large section of the canyon country along the Colorado River that was based on actual exploration.

2. In the quoted sentence, Bolton, "Pageant," p. 221, leaves out the word "almost," thus making the final clause illogical. Auerbach, "Father Escalante's Journal," p. 98, includes the word "almost."

3. The diary of the Armijo Expedition of 1829 is found in LeRoy R. and Ann W. Hafen, *The Old Spanish Trail, Santa Fe to Los Angeles* (Glendale, Calif.: Arthur H. Clark Co., 1954), pp. 158-165.

4. Timothy Flint, ed., *The Personal Narrative of James O. Pattie* (Cincinnati: John H. Wood, 1831).

5. Charles Kelly, "The Mysterious D. Julien," *Utah Historical Quarterly* 6 (1933) and Otis Marston, "Denis Julien" *Mountain Men and the Fur Trade,* 10 vols. (Glendale, Calif.: Arthur H. Clark Co., 1969), vol. 7.

4   MORMON CROSSING

1. Jacob Hamblin's missionary expeditions to the Hopis are recorded in James G. Bleak, "Annals of the Southern Utah Mission," typescript in L.D.S. Historical Department, Salt Lake City. Hamblin's autobiography is in James A.Little, *Jacob Hamblin Among the Indians* (Salt Lake City: Juvenile Instructor Office, 1881). Two biographies of Hamblin are Pearson H. Corbett, *Jacob Hamblin the Peacemaker* (Salt Lake City: Deseret Book Co., 1952), and Paul Bailey, *Jacob Hamblin, Buckskin Apostle* (Los Angeles: Westernlore Press, 1948).

2. Juanita Brooks, ed., "Journal of Thales H. Haskell," *Utah Historical Quarterly* 12, no. 1-2 (1944).

3. Bleak, "Annals."

4. C. Gregory Crampton and David E. Miller, eds. "Journal of Two Campaigns By The Utah Territorial Militia Against the Navajo Indians," *Utah Historical Quarterly* 29, no. 2 (Summer 1961).

5. Details of the 1869 farm on the Paria and of Fort Meeks are found only in Corbett, *Jacob Hamblin.* Corbett in turn cites an 1869 journal of Jacob Hamblin that was apparently owned by the Hamblin family which, if it still exists, cannot now be located.

5   MAJOR POWELL DISCOVERS LEE'S FERRY

1. Powell's highly readable report also served to spread his fame. Entitled *Exploration of the Colorado River of the West and Its Tributaries: Explored in 1869, 1870, 1871, and 1872, under the Direction of the Secretary of the Smithsonian Institution* (Washington: Smithsonian Institution, 1875), Powell's report ostensibly tells the story of the 1869 expedition only, yet events from the 1871-72 trips and from other explorations are mixed in without identification. Some recounted events are probably fictitious. For historical research, Powell's report is therefore somewhat undependable.

2. William Culp Darrah, ed., "John C. Sumner's Journal, July 6 – August 31, 1869," *Utah Historical Quarterly* 15 (1947).

3. William Culp Darrah, ed., "George Y. Bradley's Journal, May 24 – August 30, 1869," *Utah Historical Quarterly* 15 (1947).

4. Details of the 1870 expedition to the upper Paria River are found only in Lee's diary, published as Robert Glass Cleland and Juanita Brooks, eds., *A Mormon Chronicle: The Diaries of John D. Lee, 1848-1876* 2 vols. (San Marino, Calif.: Huntington Library, 1955) 2:135-141.

5. John Wesley Powell, *The Exploration of the Colorado River and its Canyons* (New York: Dover Publications, 1961), pp. 320-322.

6. Ibid., pp. 327-331.

7. Crewmember diaries from the 1871-72 expedition have been published in the *Utah Historical Quarterly* as follows: Almon Harris Thompson, 7, nos. 1, 2, 3 (January, April, July 1939); Francis Marion Bishop, 15 (1947); Stephen Vandiver Jones, John F. Steward, and W. C. Powell, 16-17 (1948-49). Frederick S. Dellenbaugh rewrote and expanded his diary, published as *A Canyon Voyage* (New Haven: Yale University Press, 1962), a reprint of the original 1908 edition. The latest diary published was Don D. Fowler, ed., *Photographed All The Best Scenery: Jack Hiller's Diary of the Powell Expeditions, 1871-1875* (Salt Lake City: University of Utah Press, 1972).

8. Dellenbaugh, *A Canyon Voyage*, p. 151.

9. Cleland and Brooks, *A Mormon Chronicle*, 2:138.

6   THE LEE OF LEE'S FERRY

1. Lee's life and character are summarized from Juanita Brooks, *John Doyle Lee, Zealot-Pioneer-Scapegoat* (Glendale, Calif.: Arthur H. Clark Co., 1962), a balanced and scholarly study.

2. A more detailed account of the "Utah War" can be found in Norman F. Furniss, *The Mormon Conflict, 1850-1859* (New Haven: Yale University Press, 1960).

3. See Juanita Brooks, *The Mountain Meadows Massacre* (Norman: University of Oklahoma Press, 1962).

4. Cleland and Brooks, *A Mormon Chronicle: The Diaries of John D. Lee*, 2:154.

5. Ibid., pp. 178-179.

6. Brooks, *John Doyle Lee*, p. 307.

7   FORGING THE VITAL LINK

1. Cleland and Brooks, *A Mormon Chronicle: The Diaries of John D. Lee,* 2:181. Although Lee does not name the *Cañon Maid,* his description fits. His description would not fit any of Major Powell's river boats, which were cached at the time at Lee's Ferry.

2. Further identification of the *Cañon Maid* can be surmised from Parker's reference to it as "Jac. Hamblin's Boat," (Cleland and Brooks, *A Mormon Chronicle,* 2:185). Powell could have given the craft to Hamblin when the two used it as a ferryboat in 1870.

3. Cleland and Brooks, *A Mormon Chronicle,* 2:196-197.

4. Ibid., pp. 208-209.

5. Dellenbaugh, *A Canyon Voyage,* p. 212.

6. Cleland and Brooks, *A Mormon Chronicle,* 2:219.

7. The history and early use of Lee's Ferry by Mormons as well as the colonization of the Little Colorado River country may be found in James H. McClintock, *Mormon Settlement in Arizona, A Record of Peaceful Conquest of the Desert* (Phoenix: Manufacturing Stationers, 1921). A summary of early expeditions to Arizona, as well as the use of Lee's Ferry, appears in Charles S. Peterson *Take Up Your Mission: Mormon Colonizing Along the Little Colorado River, 1870-1890* (Tucson: University of Arizona Press, 1973).

8. Cleland and Brooks, *A Mormon Chronicle,* 2:232.

9. Ibid., p. 240.

10. Andrew Amundsen, "Journal of a Mission to the San Francisko Mountains, Commenced March 26th 1873," manuscript in L.D.S. Historical Department, Salt Lake City.

11. Cleland and Brooks, *A Mormon Chronicle,* 2:312.

8   LEE'S FERRY FORT

1. Probably the best account of the 1874 shooting of Navajos in Grass Valley appeared in Peter Gottfredson, *History of Indian Depredations in Utah* (Salt Lake City: Skelton Publishing Co., 1919), pp. 330-332.

2. John R. Young, "The Navajo and Moqui Mission," *Improvement Era* 17, no. 3 (Jan. 1914).

3. Lee's role in the 1874 Navajo uprising appears in his diary, Cleland and Brooks, *A Mormon Chronicle* 2:320-323.

4. See Little, *Jacob Hamblin Among the Indians,* which is Hamblin's autobiography. Hamblin's highly colored account of his meeting with Navajos in early February 1874, and of the meeting's aftermath, appear to be self-justifications.

5. Young, "The Navajo and Moqui Mission."

6. Reprinted in Corbett, *Jacob Hamblin, the Peacemaker,* p. 374.

7. Bleak, "Annals of the Southern Utah Mission."

8. The intervention of Navajo Agent W.F.M. Arny is discussed in Lawrence R. Murphy, *Frontier Crusader—William F.M. Arny* (Tucson: University of Arizona Press, 1972), and in Frank McNitt, *The Indian Traders* (Norman: University of Oklahoma Press, 1962).

9. Alfred F. Whiting, "John D. Lee and the Havasupai," *Plateau* 21, no. 1 (July 1948).

10. *Arizona Sentinel,* 28 November 1874. Microfiche at Arizona State University, Arizona Historical Foundation, Tempe.

11. Details of Lee's trials and his execution are taken from Brooks, *John Doyle Lee.*

9   ON TO ARIZONA

1. Jackson's death is in Bleak, "Annals of the Southern Utah Mission."

2. Details on Warren Johnson, his families, and their long tenure at Lee's Ferry were obtained from interviews with the late Frank Johnson of St. George, Utah. Other descendents of Warren Johnson also provided information. A brief but valuable article is P.T. Reilly, "Warren Marshall Johnson, Forgotten Saint," *Utah Historical Quarterly* 39, no. 1 (Winter 1971).

3. Lee's Ferry file, Historical Department, L.D.S. Church, Salt Lake City.

4. Accounts of the accident appear in Little, *Jacob Hamblin,* and in the Lee's Ferry file of the Historical Department, L.D.S. Church.

5. Will C. Barnes, "The Honeymoon Trail, *Arizona Highways* 10 (Dec. 1934).

10   OUTLAW GANGS

1. See Harvey Hardy, "A Long Ride with Matt Warner," *Frontier Times,* October-November 1964, and Matt Warner, *The Last of the Bandit Riders,* as told to Murray E. King (New York: Bonanza Books, 1940).

2. Primary source for details of the robbery, the chase, and the final capture is Ralph Keithley, *Buckey O'Neill* (Caldwell, Idaho: Caxton Printers, Ltd., 1949).

3. Barnes recounts his involvement in Will Croft Barnes, *Apaches & Longhorns* (Los Angeles: Ward Ritchie Press, 1941).

11   ZANE GREY MEETS JIM EMETT

1. Reilly, "Warren Marshall Johnson, Forgotten Saint."

2. Zane Grey, "The Man Who Influenced Me Most," *American* 102, no. 2 (August 1926).

3. Andrew Karl Larson, *"I Was Called to Dixie: The Virgin River Basin: Unique Experiences in Mormon Pioneering* (Salt Lake City: Deseret News Press, 1961) pp. 238, 243.

4. A. M. McOmie, G. G. Jacobs, and O. C. Bartlett, *The Arizona Strip—Report of Reconnaissance of the Country North of the Grand Canyon* (Phoenix: Arizona Board of Control, 1915).

5. District Court Criminal Trial No. 294. Record now at Superior Court, Flagstaff, Arizona.

6. Zane Grey's first major book about the West was a biographical treatment of Buffalo Jones. See Zane Grey, *Last of the Plainsmen* (New York: Outing Publishing Co., 1908). More detail on Buffalo Jones and on the "cattalo" experiment in House Rock Valley is in Robert Easton and Mackensie Brown, *Lord of Beasts: The Saga of Buffalo Jones* (Tucson: University of Arizona Press, 1961).

7. Grey, "The Man Who Influenced Me Most."

8. Ibid.

9. "History of Lees Ferry," *Coconino Sun,* Flagstaff. Excerpts from an address by F.M. Gold. Clipping in the James McClintock file, Phoenix Public Library, Phoenix. Date not shown—probably about 1928.

12   THE ENGINEER—ROBERT B. STANTON

1. Primary sources for information on the railroad survey are Robert Brewster Stanton, *Down the Colorado,* ed. Dwight L. Smith (Norman: University of Oklahoma Press, 1965), and Robert Brewster Stanton, "Field Notes of Denver, Colorado Canyon & Pacific Railroad Survey," Microfilm copy at Utah State Historical Society, Salt Lake City.

2. Stanton's detailed railroad building proposal appeared as Robert Brewster Stanton, "Availability of the Cañons of the Colorado River of the West for Railway Purposes," *Transactions of the American Society of Civil Engineers* No. 26 (April 1892), pp. 283-361.

3. C. Gregory Crampton and Dwight L. Smith, eds. *The Hoskaninni Papers: Mining in Glen Canyon, 1897-1902* (Salt Lake City: University of Utah, 1961) Anthropological Papers No. 54.

4. C. Gregory Crampton, *Historical Sites in Glen Canyon—Mouth of San Juan River to Lee's Ferry* (Salt Lake City: University of Utah, 1960) Anthropological Papers No. 46.

13   THE PROMOTER—CHARLES H. SPENCER

1. Albert H. Jones, "Spencer Mining Operations on the San Juan River and in Glen Canyon," original manuscript in possession of W. L. Rusho.

2. Arthur C. Waller to W. L. Rusho, 15 November 1962.

3. Jones, "Spencer Mining Operations."

4. Interview with Charles H. Spencer, 22 August 1962.

5. Arthur C. Waller to W. L. Rusho, 27 March 1965.

6. Interview with Albert Leach, Kanab, Utah, 18 February 1961.

7. Interview with Charles H. Spencer, 22 August 1962.

8. Interview with Albert Leach, 23 October 1962.

9. Interview with Charles H. Spencer, 22 August 1962.

10. Interview with Bill Wilson, Clarkdale, Ariz. 24 September 1961.

11. Ibid.

12. Testimony of Jeremiah Johnson in United States v. Utah, (Supreme Court of the United States, No. 14, October Term, 1929). *Abstract in Narrative Form of the Testimony Taken Before the Special Master,* 2 vols. (Washington: Government Printing Office, 1931), copy at Utah State Historical Society, Salt Lake City.

13. Interview with Frank Johnson, St. George, Utah, 28 October 1962.

14. Interview with Albert Leach, 18 February 1961.

15. Interview with Arthur C. Waller, 28 September 1962.

16. Interview with Frank Johnson, 28 October 1962.

17. "History of Lee's Ferry," *Coconino Sun,* McClintock file, Phoenix Public Library.

18. Jones, "Spencer Mining Operations."

19. Interview with Charles H. Spencer at Paria ghost town, Utah, 22 August 1962.

20. Crampton, "Historical Sites in Glen Canyon."

21. David Allen Phoenix, *Geology of the Lees Ferry Area, Coconino County, Arizona* (Washington: Government Printing Office, 1963), U.S. Geological Survey Bulletin 1137.

14   THE DAM BUILDERS

1. John Wesley Powell, "The Irrigable Lands of the Arid Region," *Century Illustrated Monthly Magazine* 39 (1890):766-776.

2. E. C. LaRue, *Colorado River and Its Utilization* (Washington: Government Printing Office, 1916) U.S. Geological Survey Water Supply Paper 395.

3. See Sheet A, Plan and Profile of Colorado River from Lees Ferry, Ariz. to Black Canyon, Ariz.-Nev. and Virgin River, Nev., U.S. Geological Survey, 1924.

4. Records of the U.S. Geological Survey, Denver, Colorado.

5. E. C. LaRue, *Water Power and Flood Control of Colorado River Below Green River, Utah* (Washington: Government Printing Office, 1925) U.S. Geological Survey Water Supply Paper 556.

6. Ibid.

7. U.S. Bureau of Reclamation, *The Colorado River: A Comprehensive Report on the Development of the Water Resources of the Colorado River Basin for Irrigation, Power Production, and Other Beneficial Uses in Arizona, California, Colorado, Nevada, New Mexico, Utah and Wyoming* (Washington: Government Printing Office, 1946).

15   LAST DAYS OF THE FERRY

1. *Coconino Sun,* Flagstaff, Arizona, 21 November 1919, from file at Northern Arizona University, Flagstaff.

2. *Coconino Sun,* Flagstaff, Arizona, 20 July 1923, McClintock file, Phoenix Public Library.

3. *Daily News,* Denver, 19 November 1870, from files of Otis Marston, San Francisco, Calif.

4. Chief Engineers Report, signed by M. T. Burgess, Chief Engineer, Arizona Northern Railway, 21 December 1881. From file of Denver & Rio Grande Western Railroad, Colorado Historical Society, Denver.

5. Ralph A. Hoffman, "Bridging the Grand Canyon of Arizona," *Arizona Highways* 3, no. 8 (November 1927).

6. Ibid.

7. W. R. Hutchins, "Hardships Encountered In Bridging The Grand Canyon," *Arizona Highways* 5 (1929).

8. Interview with Frank Johnson, 28 October 1962.

9. Hutchins, "Hardships Encountered In Bridging The Grand Canyon."

10. *Coconino Sun,* Flagstaff, Arizona, 15 June 1928, from file at Northern Arizona University.

11. *Coconino Sun,* Flagstaff, Arizona, 21 June 1929, from file at Northern Arizona University.

12. Heber J. Grant to James H. McClintock, 15 February 1929, McClintock file, Phoenix Public Library.

13. Unidentified newspaper account, McClintock file, Phoenix Public Library.

16   GATEWAY TO THE CANYONS

1. Otis Marston, "River Runners: Fast Water Navigation," *Utah Historical Quarterly* 28, no. 3 (July 1960). Marston lists the Green and Colorado River boating parties through Utah after the Powell exploration.

2. Barry M. Goldwater, *Delightful Journey Down the Green & Colorado Rivers* (Tempe, Arizona: Arizona Historical Foundation, 1970). Senator Goldwater's book includes a listing by Otis Marston of the first hundred persons to traverse the Grand Canyon by boat.

3. Interview with Art "Bill" Greene, Jr., Wahweap Lodge, Lake Powell, 5 October 1973.

INDEX

124

Pattie, James Ohio, 13
Pete (Spencer's mule), 68, 95
Pipe Springs, 22
Pope, Muriel, 73
Powell, John Wesley, 18-24, 31-34, 74, 81, 84, 85, 105
Powell's 1869 Expedition, 6, 98
Prescott, Arizona, 53
Pueblos, prehistoric culture, 8, 9

Rainbow Bridge, 87, 88
Richards, Henry, 60
Richfield, Utah, 54, 57
Richmond, William, 85
Rio Santa Teresa, see Paria River
Roosevelt, Theodore, 5
Roundy, Lorenzo W., 35, 47
Rusho, W. L., 105

St. George, Utah, 14, 26, 31, 34, 38, 41, 49, 97
San Benito Salsipuedes, 11, 100
San Francisco Peaks, 23, 35, 43
San Juan River, 63, 87
San Juan River Canyon, 63
Santa Clara, Utah, 14
Santa Fe, 11, 12, 76
Saunders, B. F., 57
Schneider, "Rip Van Winkle," 70
Shinarump Formation, 47, 48, 107
Shivwits Indians, 22
Shivwits Plateau, 20
Skutumpah, settlement, 44
Smith, George A., 29
Smith, George A., Jr., 16
Smith, John J., 51, 52, 53, 54
Smith, "Smithy," 70
Snow, Erastus, 46
Soap Creek, 88
Soap Creek Rapids, 33, 60
Southern California Edison Company, 77, 102
Sparks, Tony Lee, 89
Spencer, Charles H., 42, 43, 63-74, 77, 95, 96, 106
Spencer Trail, 68, 94, 95
Staker, Sadie, 55
Stanton, Robert B., 59-63, 84, 97, 102
Stanton Road, 95, 102

Stiren, Bill, 51, 52, 53
Stokes, William, 43
Sumner, Jack, 6, 20, 98
Sweat, Josh, 49, 50

Thompson, Almon Harris, 23, 24
Tonalea, Arizona, 16
Tuba City, Arizona, 49, 54, 106
Tuba, Hopi Chief, 40

Utah-Arizona Road, 49
Utah Lake, 11
Ute Indians, 10, 14, 39, 65, 106
Ute Ford, see Crossing of the Fathers
Ute Trail, 20

VT Ranch, 61
Vasey's Paradise, 61
Vélez de Escalante, Fray Francisco, 6, 10, 11, 12, 13, 14, 15, 18, 98, 99
Vermilion Cliffs, 9, 15, 24, 37, 73, 98
Vernal, Utah, 50
Violet Louise, boat, 69
Virgin River, 11, 14

Wahweap Canyon, 53
Wahweap Creek, 12, 88
Wahweap Lodge, 12, 88
Wahweap Marina, 12
Warm Creek, 65, 67, 68, 69, 70, 71, 96
Warm Creek Canyon, 68, 95
Warner, Matt, 49, 50
Waters, Frank, 6
Weaver, Leo, 100
Wells, Daniel H., 46
Westwater Books, 75
White Mesa, 12
Willow Tanks, 53
Wingate Formation, 63, 65

Yavapai County, Arizona, 51, 52, 54
Yellowstone National Park, 58
Young, Brigham, 14, 15, 20, 22, 24, 26, 29, 31, 34, 40, 41
Young, John R., 41
Young, Joseph W., 37

Zuni Pueblo, New Mexico, 12